AIR VANGUARD 1

ALLISON-ENGINED P-51 MUSTANG

MARTYN CHORLTON

First published in Great Britain in 2012 by Osprey Publishing,
Midland House, West Way, Botley, Oxford, OX2 0PH, UK
44–02 23rd St, Suite 219, Long Island City, NY 11101, USA

A CIP catalog record for this book is available from the British Library

Print ISBN: 978 1 78096 151 4
PDF e-book ISBN: 978 1 78096 152 1
EPUB e-book ISBN: 978 1 78096 153 8

Index by Michael Forder
Typeset in Deca Sans and Sabon
Originated by PDQ Digital Media Solutions Ltd, Suffolk UK
Printed in China through Bookbuilders

12 13 14 15 16 10 9 8 7 6 5 4 3 2 1

www.ospreypublishing.com

Osprey Publishing is supporting the Woodland Trust, the UK's leading
woodland conservation charity, by funding the dedication of trees.

CONTENTS

ALLISON-ENGINED
P-51 MUSTANG

INTRODUCTION

The North American P-51 Mustang has a well-deserved reputation as one of the finest all-round fighter aircraft of World War II. Its creation owes a great deal to British rather than American requirements and it was the RAF (Royal Air Force) that first reaped the benefits of the fighter. The combination of a laminar flow wing and a fuselage designed to minimise drag, the Mustang was described by a US Senate Committee as being the nation's most aerodynamically perfect pursuit plane.

Ironically, the eventual largest customer of all variants of the Mustang, the USAAC (United States Army Air Corps) was not interested in NAA's (North American Aviation) private venture, which was specifically ordered for the use of the RAF in 1940. It was quite content at the time with the P-40 Warhawk and it was not until later that the USAAC saw the potential of the Mustang. This was still not fully exploited and the Allison-Mustang found itself operating in the ground-attack, dive-bombing and reconnaissance roles, restricted only by the engine's performance at higher altitudes.

The Mustang's creation is just as remarkable as the career the fighter enjoyed through World War II and for many years afterward. Its development by a company that only had a single, albeit successful, training aircraft under its belt was incredible, although a few spin-off designs from the NA-16 Harvard, including the NA-50A of which just 13 were sold to Peru, did give NAA the motivation to continue exploring fighter route. This is clearly testament to the talented people that had come together, just at the right moment, to create an aircraft that was far superior to any other at the time. NAA's inexperience in designing fighter aircraft ironically created a fresh approach that was uninfluenced by any other machine. All new advances, especially in aerodynamics, were explored where many competitors stuck with what they knew and fell behind.

The most significant factor against NAA actually succeeding was the short timescale. After opening negotiations with the British in early 1940 without even a design on the board, the company received the go-ahead to proceed in April and by May had a healthy order on the books. On the day the prototype NA-73X first flew, the British gave NAA a second order and, before the first aircraft flew, 620 aircraft were already in the order book. In the space of just six years, the company had grown from a workforce of only 75 people to one of the most influential and successful aircraft manufacturers in the world.

The design was not without its flaws and the aircraft's main Achilles' heel was the engine, which lacked power above 20,000ft (lower according to RAF test figures). The arrival of the Merlin engine in 1942 would change all that but, until that day arrived, the nearly 1,600 Allison-engined Mustangs built would have to fight hard across the globe. The engine aside, the first version of the Mustang – the P-51A – was still a potent aircraft that was described by many pilots as a 'hot ship,' especially in the dive-bombing role in the guise of the A-36. Once tactics had been laid down and experience gained, the P-51A achieved success in the air combat role against both German and Japanese opponents, the latter still being fought in early 1944.

The Allison-powered Mustang was by far the best available US-built fighter option for the RAF when it was first ordered in 1940. It remained that way throughout the war, with many models in use for its entirety and beyond. One example was AG346, the first Mustang delivered to the RAF, which was still in service on D-Day with 168 Squadron, only to be shot down near Grace, France on August 20, 1944. In fact, many Allison Mustangs actually served longer with the RAF than their Merlin-powered counterparts.

All in all, the NA-73X and the subsequent Allison marks paved the way for an aircraft that reached legendary status.

DESIGN AND DEVELOPMENT

The NA-73X – birth of a legendary fighter

A great deal of myth and legend surrounds the birth of one of the world's greatest single-seat fighters. Questions and debate continue as to the origins of the design more than 70 years after the first flight of the NA-73X, which the world later came to know as the North American P-51 Mustang.

The story begins in April 1938 when the British Air Ministry despatched a British Air Commission to the USA led by Sir Henry Self. Its task was to explore the possibilities of purchasing military aircraft, since the RAF was rapidly expanding in response to events occurring in mainland Europe. In order to save valuable time, the Air Ministry decided to look across the Atlantic. Even though the USA was adopting a strict policy of neutrality, there was nothing to prevent friendly foreign countries from buying military products, American aircraft manufacturers were leaders in several techniques of metal airframe construction and those designs that had been seen in Europe had received a great deal of praise.

"As clean as a hound's tooth!" The North American NA-73X, the founding father of the long and successful Mustang line. (NAA)

5

A tour by the commission was made throughout North America with visits to every airframe and engine manufacturer of significance, all of whom were very keen to do business. All of the companies visited by the British commission presented themselves well but it was the Lockheed Aircraft Corporation and NAA, both located in California, that were selected. Lockheed won an order for 200 light bomber and reconnaissance Hudsons and NAA an order for 400 NA-16 tandem-seat trainers. The RAF adopted the name Harvard Mk I for the latter. Within four months of placing the order, the first Harvard had arrived on British soil, which was no mean feat considering the long sea journey that had to be made from California, via the Panama Canal and across the Atlantic. The Harvard was a huge success for NAA and quickly taught the company, only formed in 1934, how to mass-produce aircraft. It also established NAA as a major manufacturer almost overnight and the newly-built factory in Inglewood, California was a hive of activity during the following months.

NAA started out as a holding company for several different aviation companies owned by the financier Clement Keys and associates. This group of businessmen had the foresight to purchase several interests in the majority of major US aircraft manufacturers, component manufacturers and some very promising airlines. These included Douglas, Curtiss, Sperry Gyroscopes, Ford Instruments, Eastern Airlines and Trans-Western Airlines. Later, General Motors purchased a stake in NAA and, following a reorganisation, the new manufacturing concern was headed by James H. 'Dutch' Kindelberger who used to work as an engineering executive for Douglas. Kindelberger had a brilliant engineering brain, having served for six years with the Glenn L. Martin Company before moving to Douglas. He was also a good businessman and his down-to-earth manner made him a very easy character to work with. A brand new factory was built at Inglewood, near Los Angeles, and personnel were selected from manufacturers within the old group. These were mainly chosen from the General Aviation Manufacturing Corporation, a company that started out building Fokker aircraft at Baltimore, Maryland.

The North American NA-16, the very first aircraft designed and built by NAA, which would evolve into the AT-6 Harvard/Texan family of trainers. A total success story from day one, the trainer went on to serve across the globe with over 15,000 built. (Author's Collection)

The failed successor of the Curtiss P-40 was the Donovan R. Berlin-designed XP-46A, which attempted to incorporate as many "modern" features as possible. The result was an unattractive aircraft that failed to perform better than the aircraft it was intended to replace. (Author's Collection)

As the beginning of World War II approached, the British and French governments were desperate for combat aircraft and both looked across the ocean for additional hardware. When the invasion of Poland occurred on September 1, 1939, both Britain and France honored their prewar agreements to declare war on Germany. An arms embargo by the USA was brought into force immediately but the President, Franklin D. Roosevelt, along with a large proportion of the Senate and Congress, was not comfortable with the original draconian measure. The US government quickly modified the original bill to allow foreign powers to purchase arms for cash only if they were taken from the country in their own vessels.

Within days, France had placed a large order for the Curtiss Mohawk, while Britain ordered the Curtiss P-40 and the Bell P-39 Airacobra. The P-39 order, which after the fall of France in the spring of 1940 was taken over by the British Direct Purchase Commission (BDPC), only actually amounted to 50 aircraft, as the larger original order was cancelled owing to the aircraft not performing as expected. By April 1940, over 10,000 aircraft were on order from a host of US manufacturers, resulting in the biggest expansion the industry has ever seen.

It was clear that the RAF, which was now alone in defending the shores of Great Britain, needed a more dedicated fighter to complement the Hawker Hurricane and Supermarine Spitfire that were already in mass production. In America, the BDPC representative in 1939 was again Sir Henry Self and his main, and high priority, task was to source the production of a new fighter.

By early spring 1940, the BDPC team had completed a comprehensive study of all of the US pursuit aircraft. There was no problem with the construction standards of any of them but, with regard to performance, they were all a little lacking. Military equipment was also insufficient and generally falling short of RAF standards at the time. The Curtiss P-40 stood out as the best, as it was maneuverable and had a top speed of 340mph between 12,000ft and 15,000ft. However, the staff of the BDPC was well aware of the limitations of the Allison engine, which without a supercharger was a poor performer above 15,000ft.

President of the North American Aviation Company, James H. "Dutch" Kindelberger (left), and his vice-president, John Leland Atwood, in formal pose in 1942. "Dutch" became NAA's president and general manager in 1934 when the company was first formed. Later promoted to chairman in 1948, he remained in this position until his death in July 1962. (NAA)

Sir Henry Self already had a good working relationship with 'Dutch' Kindelberger in terms of Harvard production, which was extended to more aircraft on the outbreak of war. With regard to the P-40, NAA was already at full capacity producing the fighter for the USAAC. This would mean that it would be several months before any P-40s reached Britain, so the BDPC had no alternative but to look for a second source of production. Coincidentally, Kindelberger offered the BDPC its latest new twin-engined bomber, which would go on to become the highly successful B-25 Mitchell. At the same time, in an effort to divert more P-40s to Britain, a delegation led by Self in January 1940 proposed NAA could build the Curtiss fighter under license for the RAF.

Rather than reject the notion out of hand, NAA responded with a remarkable proposal. After discussing various ideas, Kindelberger approached his chief designer, Edgar Schmued, and said, "Ed, do we want to build P-40s here?" Schmued, who had been waiting for this opportunity, responded by saying, "Well, Dutch, don't let us build an obsolete airplane, let's build a new one. We can design and build a better one." This statement was partly prompted by the problems NAA foresaw in adapting the P-40 to its own production methods, and, possibly more significantly, by personal pride in the company's ability to design a better aircraft.

 NA-73X

The NA-73X prototype N19998 which as it would have appeared when it was rolled out of North American's Inglewood factory in California on September 9, 1940. The NA-73X carried out its first flight in the hands of Vance Breese.

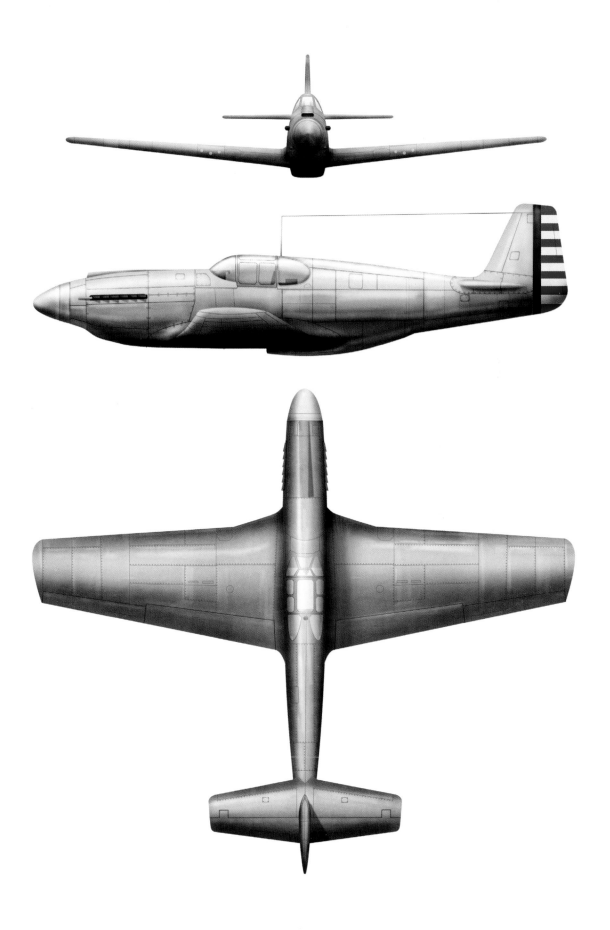

Time was of the essence, as Kindelberger was worried that Britain could not afford to wait. Kindelberger and his vice-president, British-born John Leland Atwood, travelled to New York to present Self with NAA's proposal. In typical no-nonsense style, Kindelberger described how NAA would design a single-seat fighter from the ground up, using the same Allison engine fitted in the Curtiss fighter. The most significant difference between the two fighters would be that the NAA machine would have superior performance because of an extremely low-drag airframe. NAA would also design the aircraft for current mass production techniques to ensure a rapid build.

The BDPC was most impressed with the proposal and gave Kindelberger the go-ahead for a preliminary design study. This was the only moment of caution by the BDPC, which was aware of NAA's inexperience in the design and mass production of a single-seat fighter. NAA's only previous experience was the application of a more powerful engine and a few machine guns to a heavily modified Harvard, at the same time as conversion to a single-seat model. The BDPC's decision to take the idea to design study stage displayed a lot of confidence in Kindelberger.

NAA designs and builds a fighter

The ball started rolling almost instantly after Kindelberger sent a telegram back to his designers at Inglewood on April 24, 1940. Chief of engineering Raymond Rice and assistant chief design engineer Edgar Schmued both immediately set their respective teams to work, despite it being a Saturday.

Larry L. Waite (left), aerodynamicist, Raymond H. Rice (centre), chief of engineering, and Edgar Schmued, chief designer, strike an uncomfortable pose over a set of Mustang drawings. Like Kindelberger, Schmued was also German-born. His talent did not end with the P-51, as he also went on to design the iconic F-86 and F-100. (NAA)

Kindelberger caught a flight back to California, leaving Atwood behind in New York to continue negotiations. At Inglewood, the design teams continued working through the night on general arrangement drawings and a preliminary weight study, all in time for Kindelberger to view the results by 10 am on April 25. The design at this stage was provisionally known as the NA-50B. As promised, the drawings were delivered to Kindelberger's office and the president of NAA was very happy with what he saw. The Schmued-produced drawings presented a very sleek, low-wing monoplane with every effort incorporated to keep drag to a minimum. The design was simple yet functional and Kindelberger felt confident that the British would be pleased.

The new aircraft would be built around the Allison V-1710 water-cooled 12-cylinder inline Vee engine, which was already used in the P-40, but with greater range and performance. In 1938, Kindelberger was lucky enough to visit both the Heinkel and Messerschmitt factories, taking detailed notes on the production of liquid-cooled engined fighters. John Atwood was also ordered by the British to obtain (at a cost of $56,000) as much technical aerodynamic information as possible about Don Berlin's Curtiss XP-46. It was this data that has caused a great deal of unnecessary conjecture as to the design origins of the Mustang. NAA never made a secret of the purchased material and it has also transpired that the USAAC insisted that the company should have the data at its disposal as well. However it is very unlikely that any information gleaned from the XP-46 as a whole would have been of any practical assistance. The NA-73X was destined to leave the NAA as a considerably more advanced aircraft that the Curtiss machine. The Curtiss XP-46 was a scaled-down version of the P-40, incorporating many unique features such as an inward-retracting undercarriage, slotted wings, self-sealing fuel tanks, armor protection for the pilot and a radiator set below the fuselage directly under the cockpit. It was the latter feature that, externally, was the only similarity between the Curtiss design and the new NAA machine.

Atwood made several trips to the BDPC offices and was heavily involved in the negotiations, as described by the man himself.

I made several trips to New York from January to April [1940] and stayed at the Essex House most of the time. I received some assistance from the General Motors offices at 1775 Broadway, not far from the Essex House. Also, I was assisted from time to time by R. L. Burla of the NAA staff and L. T. Taylor, then based in Washington, DC for the company. A. T. Burton who had been stationed in England for the Harvard program also assisted. The Chadbourne law firm gave me legal assistance, mainly through Ralph Ray, a partner in the firm.

Only one flying prototype was ever built, but a static-test airframe, virtually replicating the NA-73X, was also created. The static-test airframe was designated the XX-73 and was used to test the airframe to breaking point, which occurred well above the design load. (NAA)

I made it clear that we had no design, but that if authorised to proceed, we would design and build the aircraft in accordance with the representations I had made to the BDPC. These conversations went on until about the last week in March or the first week in April, when apparently affirmative recommendations were made to Sir Henry Self. At that time he called me in and discussed the project and asked me for a definite proposal. He made a reservation, however, and took note of the fact that we had not ever designed an actual fighter plane. He asked me if I thought I could get copies of the wind-tunnel tests and flight tests of the P-40 airplane. He said if I could, it would increase their confidence in our ability to move forward in a timely way. I told him I would try, and that night I took a train to Buffalo where I called upon Mr Burdett Wright who was general manager of the Curtiss division at Buffalo. After negotiating with him for most of the day, I arranged to purchase copies of the wind-tunnel tests and the flight test report for the sum of $56,000, which would cover the out-of-pocket expenses and some proportion of the cost of the tests.

I went back to New York and indicated to Sir Henry that I had been able to secure the data and presented him with a draft of the letter contract, which called for the production of 320 NA-73 aircraft equipped with an Allison engine and certain armaments to be furnished by the British, and an airframe to be designed and built by NAA – the total cost to the British government excluding engine, armaments, etc., was not to exceed $40,000 per airplane.

Although some technical work was by then being done in Los Angeles, we had not at this time presented the British Purchasing Commission [BDPC] with drawings or specifications of any kind except for free-hand sketches I had used to demonstrate the concept in informal conversations, and a letter contract was the sole document available. Sir Henry Self executed this document, after having it edited by his legal staff, and with this instrument the Mustang project got under way.

The highly competent Vance Breese was, quite possibly, one of the most highly qualified test pilots of his day. He flew more than 100 different types of aircraft, including the NA-73X, which he tested for the first time on October 26, 1940. (Author's Collection)

The blueprints and design specifications of the new NA-73X were enthusiastically approved by the BDPC. The design was actually shown to the British before the data from the XP-46 was thoroughly analysed. Despite this, the Curtiss design team would accuse NAA of plagiarism, even though it was obvious that the XP-46 had its roots in the early 1930s while the NA-73X utilised many new design features.

When the British approved the design of the NA-73X, the timescale of 120 days is often quoted. This timescale is and has been subject to much discussion. Whether it was from approval of the drawings to prototype rollout, or from the date of the initial order to first flight, or a combination of the two, is unknown, but it certainly was not applied by the BDPC.

The preliminary design was approved by Sir Henry Self, Air Vice-Marshal G. B. A. Baker, and Mr H. C. B. Thomas of the Royal Aircraft Establishment (RAE) on May 4, 1940, and the first order for 320 aircraft was placed on May 29, with a price of $33,400 quoted for the basic airframe plus a further $983.95 for the engine and related accessories. Extra equipment, not including the radio and armament, gave a grand total of $37,590.45. The total cost for all 320 aircraft, including spares and crating for overseas equipment, came to $14,746,964.35. This was a bargain compared to some of the deals that the BDPC had struck with other manufacturers.

It was from this point that everyone involved in the NA-73X worked extremely hard, conscious of the pressure of the deadline. Accuracy was paramount, with every mathematical and aerodynamic calculation being made without any margin for error. The aircraft, as per Kindelberger and Atwood's wishes, was designed from the outset for massed production, and every component from the start was made with this purpose in mind. As every component was designed, an accurate wooden mock-up was produced as well, to help production plans and to show that the particular piece of equipment could be installed in the aircraft without difficulty. This also showed, at a very early stage, any snags that might occur before it was fitted into the real airframe.

Another feature of the NA-73X was the number of castings the design employed compared to European designs of the day. Many of the castings were produced by a host of specialist subcontractors, all of whom were watched over by NAA staff who would carry off the part as soon as it was completed. It was not uncommon for engineers to work throughout the night during the summer of 1940, poring over plans of the NA-73X. Over 3,000 design drawings were used to build the fighter, and, despite the apparent complexities of the project, by early August it seemed that the NA-73X would be ready ahead of schedule. The only concern was the engine, which was in great demand for the P-38, P-39, and P-40, so that not even a single unit

After Paul Balfour's crash, Robert C. Chilton took over the job of chief of flight testing. It was not until April 1941 that Chilton made his first flight in the repaired NA-73X, but from that day onwards he would go on to fly the vast majority of test flights on all Mustangs built. (Author's Collection)

appeared to be forthcoming. Consequently, NAA had to struggle with bureaucracy, and while progress was made, it was obvious that the airframe would be ready several weeks before an Allison engine could arrive. It later transpired that the delay happened because the NA-73X was officially classed as a private venture and, as such, would receive "government furnish equipment" as and when it became available.

After 78,000 engineering hours over 127 days, the NA-73X, registered NX19998, was given a ceremonial rollout on Harvard wheels, albeit minus an engine, at Mines Field, Los Angeles, on September 9, 1940. This was 102 days after the Air Ministry contract was signed. The fighter would now sit in Inglewood's Hangar No.1 until the Allison engine arrived. It was not until October 7 that a single Allison V-1710-39 (F3R) arrived. Within 24 hours, it was installed and the fighter was taxiing under its own power for the first time. Without wasting any more time, the aircraft was first flown from Mines Field on the morning of October 26, 1940 for just 20 minutes by test pilot Vance Breese.

The NA-73X was a beautiful aircraft, every inch a thoroughbred. The list of ground-breaking design features was long, but one of the most significant was the wing. Utilising information provided by the United States National Advisory Committee for Aeronautics (NACA), the NAA produced a laminar flow wing, which was designed to allow an uninterrupted flow of air over the surface.

The flight-test program was progressing nicely when Vance Breese, who was a civilian freelance test pilot, handed the NA-73X over to NAA test pilot Paul Balfour. Breese made no secret of his low opinion of Balfour's abilities, even going as far as to make a bet that he would crash the NA-73X on his first flight. Unfortunately his prophecy proved correct. While on his first familiarisation flight, Balfour crashed on approach to Mines Field on November 20, 1940. Part of the flight was to make a high-speed pass over Mines Field to test the NA-73X's speed between two timing points. After making the first high-speed pass, Balfour forgot to switch fuel tanks. After only being airborne for 12 minutes, the aircraft ran out of fuel and suddenly became

Not a line is out of place in this lovely three-quarter view of the NA-73X, only days before its first flight in October 1940. The aircraft performed as beautifully as its appearance suggests for Vance Breese but still needed care, as Balfour would find out. (NAA)

a glider. Attempting to turn towards the active runway, Balfour lost height too quickly. With its undercarriage down, the NA-73X landed in a cultivated field and, on touching the soft ground, turned over on its back trapping Balfour in the cockpit. Luckily, the machine did not catch fire, giving his rescuers time to dig him out. With just 3 hours and 20 minutes flying time under its belt, the aircraft was seriously damaged and would not be back in the air until January 1941. Schmued attempted to brief Balfour on the takeoff and flight-test procedure before Balfour flew, but he refused to listen, saying that "one airplane was like another."

By the time the NA-73X returned to the air, the flight-test program had been handed over to Robert C. "Bob" Chilton, who would continue to test all variants of the P-51 during World War II. Chilton flew the fighter for the first time on April 3, 1941 and would fly the NA-73X on another 12 occasions. Only one other NAA test pilot is recorded as flying the NA-73X before the aircraft was grounded, namely Louis Wait.

While the NA-73X was being repaired, the RAF had come up with a name for the aircraft that would be adopted universally. Having considered the name "Apache" suggested by NAA, the RAF chose "Mustang." After the US entered World War II, many pilots flying the A-36 dive-bomber version of the airplane wanted to adopt the name "Apache" to set it apart from the fighter model, which was then known as the P-51. The name was unofficially adopted, but as US forces in western Europe progressed towards Italy the name "Invader" was also suggested for the A-36 when a 27th FBG (Fighter Bomber Group) pilot said "it keeps invading places." However, despite these unofficial names associated with the A-36, the aircraft was always officially known as a "Mustang."

The NA-73X continued to operate as part of the NAA's development program until July 15, 1941, when it was grounded indefinitely. It was destined to be the only prototype of the Mustang. The only other pre-production aircraft was a static-test airframe that is occasionally referred to as the XX-73. This served its purpose by being tested to destruction in January 1941 after the wing structure failed at a point 5 percent higher than the design load.

In a field close to Mines Field lies the undignified wreckage of the once-pristine NA-73X on November 20, 1941. After being airborne for just 12 minutes after takeoff, test pilot Paul Balfour neglected to switch to the correct fuel tank, starving the engine of fuel. (NAA)

The ground-breaking prototype spent the remainder of its days at Inglewood before allegedly being donated to a school located near the NAA factory. Whatever the aircraft's fate, this innovative and beautiful machine eventually met an undignified end as scrap.

The RAF order

Within days of the swift roll-out of the North American NA-73X in September 1940, the RAF placed a second order for 300 aircraft, months before a single machine had crossed the Atlantic. Kindelberger wasted no time preparing the production lines for the order, which would give NAA almost three years of steady work. The new fighter produced very few problems during its test program and production lines were planned for the first Mustang Mk I, starting with the RAF serial AG345, to begin before the end of 1940.

AG345 was the first aircraft completed, on April 16, 1941, first flying on April 23, and was destined never to leave the hands of NAA, who retained the aircraft until it was SOC (Struck off Charge) on December 3, 1946. AG345 represented an incredible achievement as it was exactly one year previously that Sir Henry Self had given 'Dutch' Kindelberger the order to go ahead with the preliminary design.

It was the second production aircraft, AG346, which was to become the first of its kind to arrive in Britain on October 24, 1941, many months behind schedule. The Atlantic crossing would prove to be a particularly hazardous journey for all of the RAF's Mustangs, 25 of them being lost at sea because of U-boats, the majority during 1942. AG346 was delivered by road from Liverpool docks to RAF Speke (now John Lennon Airport) from where it made its first flight in early November. AG346 was later flown down to RAF Boscombe Down in Wiltshire, where it was quickly standardised with a TR.1133 radio, Mk II reflector gunsight, and British specification oxygen connectors.

AG346 made quite an impression on all of the pilots who were lucky enough to fly it. Although restricted to a service ceiling of 30,000ft, the fighter performed well and the only initial criticism was that the camouflage paint slowed the Mustang by approximately 8mph. Early test results produced healthy performance figures of 375mph at 15,000ft compared to the Spitfire

The very first Mustang to arrive in Britain was AG346, which was photographed at Speke before its first flight test in November 1941. The aircraft was the first of a batch of 320 Mustang Mk Is ordered under contract A-250, all of which were delivered (except AG345, which remained with NAA) between November 1941 and May 1942. (Author's Collection)

Mk V, which could only reach 340mph at the same height. Extensive testing of AG346 revealed that up to 20,000ft the Mustang was faster than any other fighter in service with the RAF at the time. Speed was measured at 382mph at 13,000ft, and between 7,000 and 20,000ft the Mustang was averaging up to 30mph quicker than the Spitfire. Climb rate, acceleration, dive speed, stability, general handling, rate of roll and radius of turn were recorded from being satisfactory through to outstanding. It was the range and endurance that made the Mustang stand out from other fighters of the day. The Spitfire had an average range of 400 miles and an endurance of just 2 hours, while the Mustang, even in unfamiliar hands, could stay airborne for 4 to 5 hours and cover over 1,000 miles without drop tanks!

The Mustang did not have it all its own way, as the Spitfire could reach 20,000ft in just 7 minutes while the American fighter took 11. At higher altitudes, both the Spitfire and Bf 109 were more maneuverable, and the Mustang was deemed underpowered compared to the much lighter British fighter.

P-51s fresh off the Inglewood production line are prepared for flight testing. Only FD553 can be identified in the background, wearing a combined USAAF and RAF style fin flash. The fighter went on to serve with 63 and 268 Squadrons. Its final fate is unknown. (Library of Congress)

The first Mustang Mk I to arrive at the Aeroplane and Armament Experimental Establishment (A&AEE), Boscombe Down was AG351 on November 22, 1941. Test flying did not begin until January 1942 because of engine problems which, according to one of the flight test reports, were due "to the abnormally high temperatures due to coring [engine oil congealing due to over cooling] … during the winter months, tests had to be made with various types of blanks over the oil cooler and [engine] radiator." The blanks used had quite an effect on performance, especially the maximum level speed, which was 370mph at 15,000ft without blanks and 357mph with them. It is presumed that the loss in speed was not only caused by the increased drag but also by the loss of the "jet" effect (the "Meredith Effect"). Rate of climb seemed unaffected by the blank being in place, and a climb rate of 1,980ft/min at 11,300ft was recorded.

The lack of guns under the nose and the beefy-looking 20mm cannon in the wings give this away as Mustang Mk IA, FD449. The fighter served with AST (Air Service Training) and 268 Squadron before being SOC on June 10, 1944. (Author's Collection)

All test pilots were very complimentary about the handling of AG351. "There is no appreciable tendency to swing [on takeoff]…Crosswind take-offs presented no difficulties in winds up to 25mph." In contrast, the landing was more challenging in a 25mph crosswind, "not difficult but there is barely enough aileron control to effect the required sideslip, with the tail wheel fixed [i.e. locked], as our pilots recommended. Rudder alone was necessary to check the tendency to swing into the wind after touchdown."

Another criticism was the position of the fighter's low-slung radiator, which received a substantial blast from the propeller on the ground. While this obviously aided cooling, there was also the high chance, on a loose surface, of the propeller throwing up small stones or any other loose matter. Airfields with concrete runways and dispersals were not seen as an issue, but grass airfields, such as Boscombe Down at the time, could present an operating hazard.

From May to August 1942, AG351 was used for fuel consumption trials at Boscombe Down. The aircraft was flown at an AUW (all up weight) of 8,300lb. At this weight, the still-air range of the Mustang at 15,000ft was 8.75 ampg at 180mph IAS (indicated airspeed). The results of the test were slightly marred by the fact that AG351 only had a fuel capacity of 130 imperial gallons, when all later aircraft had 140. AG351 still managed to fly for a maximum range of 990 statute miles, and had an endurance of 4.1 hours. The consumption made no allowance for combat, however, which was estimated by the A&AEE to reduce the maximum range by over 80 miles

Mustang Mk I AG351 was the first of its type to 'officially' pass through the A&AEE at Boscombe Down for flight testing. Pictured on February 9, 1942, the fighter was popular with all test pilots who were lucky enough to fly it. (Author's Collection)

Mustang Mk I AM106/G (Guard) spent its entire existence, from May 1942 to November 1944, serving as a weapons trials aircraft with the A&AEE. Much of the work carried out centered around the installation of a pair of Vickers "S" 40mm guns, which were trialled inside various pods and fairings. (Author's Collection)

for 5 minutes' use of combat boost. Of the first small batch of 20 aircraft to arrive in Britain, virtually all ended up in the hands of the A&AEE, the RAE, and the AFDU (Air Fighting Development Unit) for test and evaluation trials. It was the A&AEE that saw the most Allison-engined variants, as, including AG351 mentioned earlier, 16 Mk Is, two Mk IAs, and four Mk IIs passed through Boscombe from late 1941 through to early 1944. The last was Mk II FR932, which was used for IFF (identification friend or foe) and radio trials from January 8, 1944.

All who tested the new fighter were complimentary in many respects, but it was obvious that the aircraft's Allison liquid-cooled V-12, 1,100hp V-1710-39 was not a performer above 13,000ft. RAF Fighter Command was the intended main user of the new Mustang, but it was quickly labeled a low-level performer, which was not its area of operations. It was, however, the territory of Army Co-Operation Command, who needed to replace the unpopular Curtiss Tomahawk and who therefore found an unplanned role for the Mustang Mk I.

 B

1: XP-51 (USAAC) MARKINGS
The first of two Mustangs pulled from the first RAF production line was the fourth aircraft, serialled by the USAAC as 41-038. The aircraft arrived at Wright Field for testing on August 24, 1941 but a very busy workload meant that testing was delayed, although an order for 150 P-51s had already been placed by the Army. The aircraft survives today at Oshkosh, Wisconsin.

2: A-36A (27TH BG)
Only one Allison-powered Mustang "Ace" was created during World War II. This was Lieutenant Michael T. Russo of the 522nd FS, 27th FG in his personal aircraft, 42-83830, named "Pat." The skull and crossbones on the tail was painted on the day of his fifth victory but he was later ordered to remove it.

3: MUSTANG 1 (26 SQN)
Mustang Mk I AM148 entered RAF service with 26 Squadron at Weston Zoyland in early 1942. The fighter later served with 430 Squadron before seeing out its days with Rolls-Royce at Hucknall, being SOC on April 24, 1944.

4: P-51A (23RD FG)
A survivor of the 23rd FG's operations over China was P-51A-10 43-6298 "Lynn". The aircraft was flowvn by Captain John S. Stewart from February to May 1944.

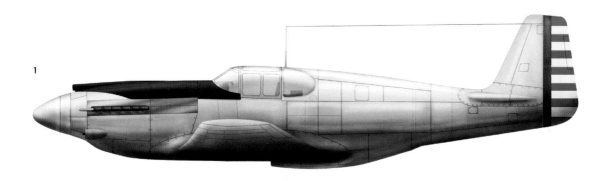

1

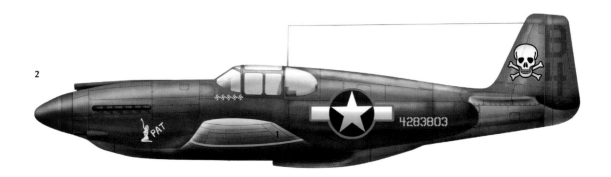

2

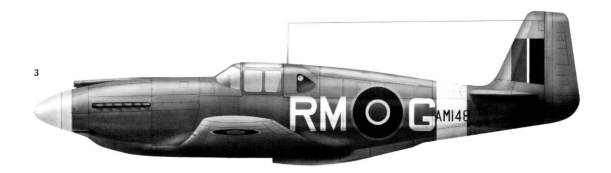

3

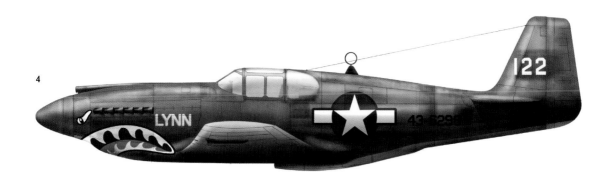

4

The USAAF shows interest

During the early stages of production, the fourth and tenth aircraft were allocated to the USAAC and designated as XP-51s on July 24, 1941. These two aircraft, 41-038 and 41-039, were selected for evaluation as part of the Army's fighter program, which was inundated with new types already put forward by Bell, Curtiss, Lockheed and Republic Aviation. The test pilots at the test-flight center at Wright Field, Ohio, were overworked testing products from companies already established in fighter types. NAA was still an unknown quantity and would have to take its turn. However, the Army did order 150 NA-91s (P-51s/Mustang Mk Is) on July 7, 1941 as part of a USAAF order well before testing began. This was on behalf of the RAF in a lend-lease deal that was viewed as a top-up order for the RAF.

During 1941 the USAAF was expanding so quickly that there was not enough money for new fighters. There was however money for attack aircraft and, after intensive discussions between the Pentagon and NAA, the Mustang was redesigned for this role. The new aircraft was designated the NA-97 and, after an order for 500 aircraft was placed on August 21, 1942, it was officially referred to as the A-36A, which was essentially a dive-bomber version of the Mustang.

The first A-36A took to the air in the hands of Ben Chilton on September 21, 1942. Power was provided by an uprated Allison V-1710-87 (F21R) engine that produced 1,325hp at 3,000ft. The aircraft was stressed for high-speed diving and a set of fence-type hydraulically operated dive brakes were fitted above and below each wing. Positioned outboard of the bomb hardpoints, the dive brakes were recessed into the wing but were opened to 90° by a hydraulic jack to hold speed in very steep dives at around the 350mph mark.

The first XP-51 41-038 (c/n 73-3101), which was taken from the production line for testing by the Army at Wright Field in July 1941. This aircraft survived the war, and after several years was restored to flight in the 1970s. The aircraft is now on static display at the Experimental Aircraft Association Museum in Oshkosh, Wisconsin. (NASA)

Armament was a pair of 0.5in. Brownings in each wing and another pair in the nose, although the latter fit was often removed in the field to save weight. A pair of racks was also fitted under each wing to carry a pair of 500lb bombs, smoke generators, or a pair of 75 US gallon drop tanks.

Flight tests were carried out at Eglin Army Air Field in Florida and it was quickly discovered that the A-36 could easily achieve a dive speed of 500mph. With the dive breaks extended this was reduced to 350mph, but unfortunately one of the early test aircraft was lost when it shed both wings in a vertical dive. This incident sowed seeds of doubt amongst some Army officials, who acknowledged that the A-36 had an excellent dive rate for a fighter but went down too fast for a dive-bomber. It was recommended that the A-36 be restricted to a dive angle of 70° and be used mainly as a low-altitude attack aircraft with the dive breaks removed. The latter recommendation was never implemented.

One of many challenges that the fledgling A-36 pilot had to face was the distinct lack of specialist training available at the time in dive-bombing techniques. A handful of USN (United States Navy) and USMC (United States Marine Corps) instructors were temporarily loaned to the Army, but generally it was an art that was initially self-taught through experience and improvisation. A distinct lack of aircraft was another problem, with many A-36 pilots only encountering the type once they were in theater as none were available during their training. Replacement aircraft were also lacking, but what the A-36 is rarely credited for is that it kept the production lines open for the Merlin engine variants that were to come later and transform the Mustang into a classic fighter.

The keen-eyed will notice the twin-landing lights before the retracted speed brakes, both of which were unique to the NA-97, more commonly known as the A-36. 500 of these dive-bombing/ground-attack machines were built, all working hard in the Mediterranean and Far East well into 1944. (USAAF)

Ex 42-83685 was the only A-36A to arrive in Britain during World War II. Reserialed as EW998, the aircraft arrived at Boscombe Down on March 10, 1943. It was prematurely SOC on July 15, 1943. (Author's Collection)

A single A-36A was trialed by the RAF at Boscombe Down in March 1943. Renamed the Mustang Mk I (Dive-Bomber), EW998 (ex 42-83685) only remained on RAF strength until July 1943. EW998 was not the only A-36 destined to serve the RAF. 1437 Flight, which had been operating reconnaissance flights from North Africa since March 1942, gained at least six ex-USAAF A-36s during 1943.

Enter the P-51A (NA-99)

It was August 1942 when the Army ordered 310 NA-99s, designated P-51A. Effectively, these aircraft were A-36As with the dive brakes and twin nose guns removed. Power was provided by an Allison V-1710-81 (F20R), which was rated at 1,125hp at 18,000ft in an effort to give better performance above 20,000ft. A more powerful supercharger was also fitted to improve the low-level performance which, combined with a new larger-diameter propeller, gave the P-51A a top speed of 409mph at 11,000ft. The P-51A at this medium height was the fastest fighter in the world and was also described by US test pilots as having "the best all-round fighting qualities of any present American fighter." Armament consisted of four 0.5in. Brownings with large magazine tanks capable of holding up to 1,260 rounds. The ability to carry a pair of 500lb bombs or a pair of drop tanks was also retained.

1: MUSTANG IA (414 SQN)
It was an American volunteer flying with the RCAF who claimed the first kill by an RAF Mustang on August 19, 1942 over Dieppe. Flying Officer Hollis H. "Holly" Hills shot down a Fw 190 in his Mk IA AG470, which only served with 414 (RCAF) Squadron until being SOC March 13, 1947.

2: MUSTANG I (2 SQN)
Mustang Mk I AG633 served with 2 Squadron at Sawbridgeworth from late 1941 until its demise on October 29, 1942. After carrying out an overshoot in poor weather at Sawbridgeworth, the fighter lost height and crashlanded.

3: F-6A (111TH TRS, 68TH TRG)
One of the 35 reconnaissance-configured P-51s that were shipped to North Africa in early 1943 and designated as the F-6A. This example, 41-37365, served with the 111th TRS, 68th TRG. The latter, originally known as the 68th OG, rightfully claimed to be the "Pioneer Mustang Group."

4: F-6B (107TH TRS, 67TH TRG)
F-6B 43-6046 of the 107th TRS, 67th TRG, displaying invasion stripes as worn whilst operating from Membury in June 1944. The group carried out a large number of dangerous low-level photographic sorties along the French coast in support of the landings on June 6, 1944.

1

2

3

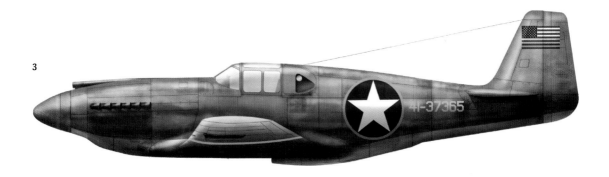

4

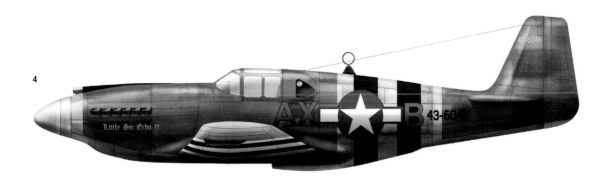

The prototype P-51A first flew on February 3, 1943. Of the 310 P-51As built, 50 were sent to England to become the Mustang II, while the remainder were despatched to India and North Africa. The first models, however, were sent to the 54th FG (Fighter Group) at Bartow Army Field, Florida, where new Mustang pilots would cut their teeth on the fighter.

Reconnaissance birds, the F-6A and F-6B

The A-36 would not be the first Mustang to enter service with the USAAF, as 55 Lend-Lease Mustang Mk IAs, destined for the RAF, had been held back. All were retrofitted with a pair of K.24 (the US version of the British F.24) cameras in the rear fuselage for tactical low-level reconnaissance and redesignated as the F-6A (although confusingly they were still referred to as the P-51 or P-51-1). All were sent to the home of the newly-established Aerial Reconnaissance School at Peterson Field, Colorado and then on to the Twelfth Air Force in Tunisia. It was from here that F-6A 41-137328 flew the USAAF's first Mustang mission of the war, a reconnaissance of Kairouan Airfield, while serving with the 154th OS (Observation Squadron).

Considering that the F-6s were originally intended for the British, it seems ironic that 225 Squadron RAF, serving in North Africa at the same time, often borrowed aircraft from 154th OS because its own Spitfires had too short a range for certain operations. The F-6A was an extremely competent aircraft, proving its worth in the reconnaissance role for the remainder of World War II. Its one drawback, especially as the type became more prolific, was recognition, since it would often be confused with the Bf 109. Unfortunately, the first combat loss from the 154th OS was caused by friendly antiaircraft fire, with fatal consequences. The first of several F-6As fell to Allied guns over

View of P-51A showing the aircraft's maximum use of straight lines, especially along the leading and trailing edges of the wing and tailplane. The structure within was also made deliberately simple to aid both speed and accuracy of construction. (Author's Collection)

North Africa on April 23, 1943, which mistook the angular shape of the Mustang for a Bf 109, despite being alerted to the new fighter being in theater.

The F-6B was little more than a P-51A fitted with the K.24 cameras in the same positions as the F-6A, and only 35 were ever built, making it a very rare bird.

The main user of the F-6 in the European theater was the 10th Photographic (later Reconnaissance) Group of the Ninth Air Force, which established its HQ at Chalgrove Airfield, Oxfordshire, in early 1944. One of its early squadrons, the 31st PRS (Photo Reconnaissance Squadron), was equipped with the F-6, which undertook many highly successful low-level reconnaissance flights over Northern France before the D-Day invasion on June 6, 1944. One of these missions, which was flown in May, earned the group a Distinguished Unit Commendation. The group's F-6 contingent was expanded from June 13, 1944 when it gained the 12th and 15th PRS from the 69th TRG (Tactical Reconnaissance Group), which was based at Middle Wallop Airfield, Hampshire, at the time. Both groups remained attached to the 67th TRG but, along with the other squadrons, served the 10th PG through to the Battle of the Bulge, the crossing of the Rhine and onward to VE-Day.

As already mentioned, the second group of the Ninth Air Force that operated the F-6 was the 67th TRG. Originally an Eighth Air Force unit, the 67th TRG was transferred in October 1943 and was made up of the 12th, 15th, 107th and 109th TRS (Tactical Reconnaissance Squadron), all of which operated the F-6 as well as the Spitfire and F-5/P-38. The HQ moved into Middle Wallop from Membury Airfield, Devon, in December 1943 and its squadrons operated from airfields in the vicinity, including Greenham Common, Aldermaston and Chalgrove, up until the Normandy landings in 1944. Operations across occupied Europe began immediately, with their aircraft flying regular reconnaissance, weather-reconnaissance and raid-assessment operations.

The final group to join the action was the 69th TRG, which did not begin training on the F-6 and the Douglas A-20 Havoc in the US until January 1945. It was moved to Nancy in northern France on March 22, 1945, and, of its four squadrons, the 10th, 22nd and 111th TRS all flew the F-6. The group flew visual operations for the remainder of the war before it returned back to the US from June 1945. The 67th TRG began the lengthy process of returning to the US from July 1945, while the now redesignated 10th RG (Reconnaissance Group) had already begun to return the previous month. It was not until November 1945 that the last Ninth Air Force F-6 squadron was inactivated, and this was probably the swan song for the F-6 family.

TECHNICAL SPECIFICATIONS

The NA-73X

The only engine available
The fuselage lines of the NAA's new fighter were dictated from the outset by the criteria of a 5ft 10in., 140lb pilot, and by the only water-cooled powerplant available at the time, the Allison V-1710. The water-cooled powerplant presented a considerably lower frontal area compared to the big air-cooled radials of the day, but also had the disadvantage of having to incorporate a complex liquid-cooling system into the design.

Following Allison becoming part of General Motors in 1929, the company invested private funds into the development of a new liquid-cooled V12 engine at the request of the general manager, Norman H. Gilman. The USAAC initially showed no interest in Allison's plans, but the USN did, seeing the new unit as a potential reversible airship engine. The first of many Allison liquid-cooled engines, the V-1710-A, was test run in 1931, delivering a promising 650hp at 2,400rpm. The original design was the same 5.5in. bore and 6.0in. stroke that would remain for all subsequent V-1710s built. Testing was completed by 1932, by which time the USAAC had finally shown an interest.

Continued development of the Allison during the early 1930s was stalled because of the Great Depression until a V-1710 flew again in a Consolidated XA-11A in December 1936. The engine then became the first to pass the USAAC's 150-hour type test successfully in April 1937, giving Allison the opportunity to offer the V-1710 to the nation's aircraft manufacturers. Coincidentally, a competition for a new pursuit fighter for the USAAC was about to take place and all three entrants, the P-38, P-39 and P-40, had been designed around the V-1710.

It was the British specification for the new fighter that dictated that the engine should be a liquid-cooled inline model. By 1940, the Allison engine of choice was the V-1710-39 (F3R), which was built for the P-40D and mass produced for the P-40E. A single engine was supplied for the NA-73X only a few weeks before the prototype first took to the air. The non-supercharged unit (only the prototype's engine was not supercharged – all subsequent Allison engine variants were fitted with a two-stage engine-driven supercharger) produced 1,120hp and was fitted into the slender fuselage by a pair of Y-shaped bearers equipped with large rubber blocks. The bearers were constructed in similar fashion to wing spars and were made from aluminum sheet. The extrusions were attached to a steel firewall at the bolted joint between the front and centre fuselage attachment points.

The Allison V-1710 was first conceived as far back as 1931 but full development did not commence until 1936. It went on to become the only US V-12 liquid-cooled engine to see service during World War II and more than 70,000 were built. (USAAF)

1. Oil Pressure Relief Valve
2. Main Oil Pump Check Valve
3. Distributor With Gun Synchronizer Drive

4. Exhaust Flanges (Without Exhaust Stacks)
5. Cowl Support Studs

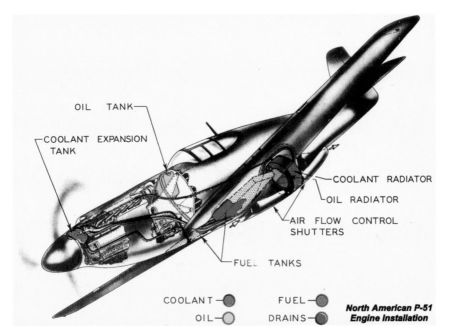

OIL TANK

COOLANT EXPANSION TANK

COOLANT RADIATOR

OIL RADIATOR

AIR FLOW CONTROL SHUTTERS

FUEL TANKS

COOLANT — ○
OIL — ○
FUEL — ○
DRAINS — ●

North American P-51
Engine Installation

The installation of the Allison engine was straightforward, while the positioning of the oil and coolant radiators obviously posed some challenges with regard to pipework. Some of the coolant pipes had to be over 20ft to reach the radiator but the performance gain over combat vulnerability was seen as a fair tradeoff. (USAAF)

The layout of the engine gave the NA-73X and all subsequent Allison-engined versions a distinctive long duct on top of the forward fuselage. The entry to the duct was set back 2ft behind the propeller and provided air for the engine's Bendix-Stromberg injection carburettors. The positioning of this duct would later prove to be a temporary developmental problem as its position was found to be too far back, causing the engine to be starved of air when certain maneuvers were carried out. It was later found that the problem was solved by moving the entrance to the carburettor duct directly behind the propeller.

All available power was transferred through a three-bladed Curtiss Electric propeller that within the hub incorporated an electric motor and reduction gearbox to alter the pitch of the blades. The entire unit had a diameter of 10ft 6in. and the ability for constant speed and feathering.

Slim semi-monocoque fuselage

The fuselage was designed with incredible care and all emphasis was on making it as slim and as aerodynamically perfect as possible. Aft of the engine, the cross section was reduced to the absolute minimum without reducing the field of vision from the cockpit, while still managing to make it one of the roomiest single-seaters around. This was partly achieved by keeping the profile of the canopy as low as possible, which seemed hardly to disrupt the line of the top of the fuselage from the nose through to the tail. In fact, the Mustang managed to achieve the smallest cross-sectional area ever put behind an Allison engine. The Mustang was also the first aircraft to have its contours determined by geometry, with all lines made up of composite circles, ellipses, hyperbolas and parabolas. This meant that every curve of the fuselage could be presented algebraically, enabling the precise layout, tooling, and production to be strictly controlled and repeated without deviation.

The issue of cooling always gave designers a headache when a liquid-cooled engine was installed, but Schmued and aerodynamic specialist Edward

Horkey came up with a novel solution. At the cost of weight and even combat vulnerability because of the long piping involved, the aircraft's radiators for both coolant and oil were grouped together in a long-profiled duct located under the rear fuselage.

Constructed in three sections, the fuselage could be easily dismantled by undoing bolts. The joint was located forward of the cockpit, sloping at a slight angle down towards the leading edge of the wing. The second joint was positioned in front of the tail wheel assembly. This sectionalised construction was deliberate for mass production, allowing each section of the aircraft to be constructed separately, complete with sub-systems, before it was filtered into a final assembly line.

Cooling system

The only way to keep a liquid-cooled engine running is obviously to keep it cool. This always involves radiators of some description, and, while many designs during the late 1930s were conventional, several new ones were trying to harness the cooling effect combined with a potential thrust effect as well. Examples of the period were the Hurricane to some extent, the Spitfire markedly more so, and the Bf 109, which in many people's eyes was the most effective. The German fighter was by far the lowest powered of the group but the later marks (F onwards) could easily breach 400mph. This was most likely attributed to a reaction known in Britain as the "Meredith Effect."

Fredrick W. Meredith, after much study of previous theories, published the elaborately titled *Note on the Cooling of Aircraft Engines with Special Reference to Radiators Enclosed in Ducts* in 1936. The theory was that the waste heat created by a piston engine when transferred through an air-flow cooling radiator would not be lost. A small amount of thrust could be created as long as the pressure at the exit of the radiator tubes was higher than the free static pressure. It was only in the late 1930s, as aircraft speeds began to rise to a sufficient level that this theory could be applied.

As mentioned earlier, the location of the radiators in the lower rear position involved a great deal of pipe work. Starting with the Prestone (glycol) coolant, the expansion tank was positioned at the top of the fuselage, forward of the engine directly behind the propeller hub. Three lines of coolant pipes travelled rearwards, one in a more direct path through the engine bulkhead, while the other two went below, joined as one. All met at a large circular coolant radiator located behind the cockpit, taking up most of the lower half of the fuselage. The oil was cooled in the same way, although it had a shorter route to travel because the 12 US gallon tank was located between the upper rear of the engine, directly in front of the main bulkhead. Both pipes were directed below the bulkhead and then rearwards to the oil radiator, which was neatly contained within the centre of the coolant radiator.

Air to cool the glycol and oil entered through a fuselage-wide scoop in which the airflow was controlled by shutters. The cold air passed through a giant radiator and exited via an adjustable radiator rear shutter, at which point, the warmer air, in theory, provided a small percentage of additional thrust. Downstream of the radiator, warm air was also diverted to the cockpit and was controlled by a large exit flap, driven by a jack located behind the pilot's seat.

Early air tests with the NA-73X found that the engine overheated, and follow-up wind-tunnel tests showed that the disturbed boundaries of air under the wing and fuselage prevented a clean flow of air from entering the air scoop.

The entrance lip of the scoop was lowered by a mere 1 in. from the bottom of the fuselage, curing the problem instantly without affecting performance.

The cockpit

The comfortable and very roomy cockpit not only gave the pilot good visibility but also good protection. The latter was provided via a reinforced bulkhead behind the seat, which doubled as a crash pylon. Fitted to this was also a substantial slab of armor to protect the pilot from the rear. The seat was spring-mounted and the control column was fitted with a US-style handgrip rather than a British spadegrip type. Another American feature that was retained was the operation of the brakes, which were pedal-mounted.

The canopy was made up of two fixed windows on the starboard side and, on the port, a second pair, the front one of which could slide to open so that it could be hinged outwards and downwards for access. A transparent rook panel was also hinged and opened to starboard. A flat five-ply bulletproof front windscreen that sloped at 40° was also incorporated to meet RAF requirements.

Visibility was found, especially by British pilots, to be better than that of the Spitfire, although the low line of the canopy made the legs of taller pilots a little cramped even with the seat in its lowest position. The general layout of the cockpit was excellent, with throttle controls and all other major levers and switches well placed for operation by the pilot's left hand, while the right was free to hold the control column.

A semi-empirical venture – the 'laminar flow' wing

The design of the NA-73X hinged around state-of-the-art aerodynamics, which brought about an aircraft that was described by many as "clean as a hound's tooth." The wing, fuselage, and even the cooling system were considerably more advanced than any other design of the time.

The most significant of these designs was the wing, which was laminar flow. The design, which originated from the NACA-23 Series Airfoil later redesignated as the NAA/NACA 45-100, came from the aerodynamics department of NAA, led by Larry L. Waite. Full credit for the wing was given to NACA by the NAA from the start, although by the time it had been perfected for the NA-73X the design differed markedly from the original. The idea to use it for the NA-73X came from Edward Horkey, one of the many aerodynamic specialists employed by the company.

The term "laminar flow" means that the surface was incredibly smooth, allowing for completely uninterrupted airflow over the wing in flight. When the flow of air is disrupted over the wing, turbulence is created, resulting in a loss of lift and a large amount of drag. A wing designed for minimum drag and a constant flow over the boundary layer (first discovered by German aerodynamicist Ludwig Prandtl in 1904) is known as a laminar airflow wing.

The theory was that the wing should have a symmetrical airfoil cross section, i.e. both the upper and lower surfaces would have the same curvature. The wing was very thin at the leading edge, slowly widening to its point of maximum thickness at a position as far aft as possible. In the case of the NA-73X wings, the maximum thickness point was almost halfway back, whereas a traditional wing would be approximately one-fifth of the distance from the leading edge. The laminar flow theory was that using an airfoil of this design should maintain the attachment of the boundary layers of airflow, always present in flight, as far aft as possible.

Prior to the NA-73X, there had been a few bespoke attempts at producing a laminar flow wing. However, the exacting tolerances and requisite smoothness needed had not been achieved, resulting in many manufacturers abandoning the idea because of the cost in tooling to build a mass-produced aircraft. The NAA engineers viewed the problem from a different angle. While there was still no technique available to build a wing straight off the production line, the wing could be filed and the surface painted to produce the required effect.

The whole fighter was a purely math-based design, relying more on algebra than the sweep of a designer's pencil. The NA-73X's wings were classified as a "semi-empirical venture" and were cleared by the British to be used in the design. The wing would be the only part of the aircraft actually tested in a wind tunnel. There was quite a lot of speculation surrounding the design and whether it would actually work. Very early experiments had shown that it performed well, with the expected low drag and good lift qualities. It was however very vulnerable to even the smallest of scratches or indentations and showed poor performance in the low speed ranges. A quarter-sized wing made of mahogany was made and finished to .001in. tolerances, and was wind-tunnel tested by the California Institute of Technology. The wing was found to have the lowest drag coefficient of any so far tested in the USA but evidence was found of a very bad stalling characteristic. This potential problem resulted in the engineering department making preparations for a more conventional design, to be made available within 30 days of the wind-tunnel test being carried out, just in case the laminar flow did not live up to expectations. The laminar wing was slightly modified and tested again, but still produced the same disappointing traits. Further study revealed that turbulence at the wing tips indicated that the quarter-scale wing was too big for the wind tunnel. The test team then took the model wing to the largest wind-tunnel facility in the country in Seattle, Washington. With great relief, the design team found that the wing tip turbulence had virtually disappeared. The airfoil that

1: A-36 BOMBS

A 500lb bomb mounted on a later style rack under the port wing of an A-36A.

2: A-36 GUNS

The starboard gun ports for a pair of 0.5in Browning machine guns of an A-36A.

3: LONG-RANGE DROP TANK

The RAF tested a special long-range drop tank on Mustang I AM106 during 1943.

4: NAPALM

A complicated napalm rack as tested by the RAF's AFDU (Air Fighting Development Unit) on a Mustang I. It was later used in service by the Mustang III.

5: NOSE MACHINE GUNS

Protruding barrels of the two 0.5in Browning machine guns, fitted under the nose of the Mustang I.

6: RP ROCKETS

A rack of four RPs (Rocket Projectiles) on zero-length launchers which were successfully tested on Mustang I AM106.

7: VICKERS CLASS S

AM106 was once again used to trial a pair of Vickers 'Class S' 40mm cannon on under-wing mountings.

8: WING AUTOCANNON

A pair of 20mm Hispano Mk II autocannon as fitted to the Mustang II.

9: WING GUNS

Staggered layout of three out of the six 0.5in Browning machine guns as fitted to the A-36.

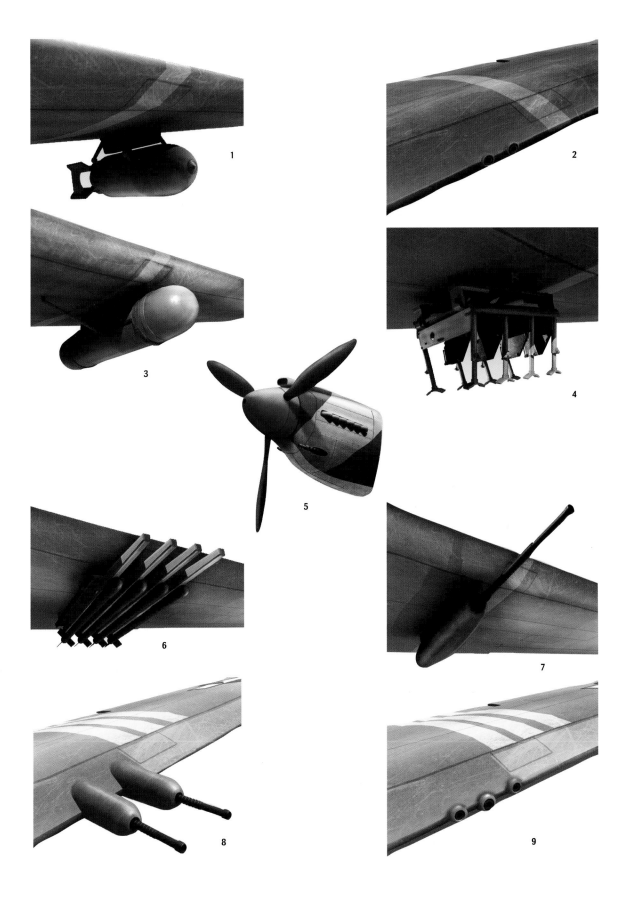

was chosen for the NA-73X had a thickness ratio of 15.1 percent at the wing root and 39 percent at the chord. The tip ratio was 11.4 percent at the 50 percent chord line.

It is worth noting that the "Davis" airfoil that was fitted to the Consolidated B-24 Liberator was also a laminar flow wing, first flown in late 1939. This was not intentional, as although the designers knew they had created a wing with very low drag, they were not aware that they had actually made a laminar flow wing.

The new fighter's wing area was only just over 233 square feet which, to put it in context, was nearly 9 square feet less than a Spitfire. This lack of wing area meant that, to make it work to its best, very large slotted flaps would have to be fitted, and these large panels, which stretched to over half the length of each wing, were a prominent feature on all Mustangs.

Construction of the wing was made as simple as possible, as per the rest of the aircraft, to make mass production as painless an exercise as possible. The wing was of cantilever stressed-skin construction and was built in port and starboard halves, both joining at the centerline. The spars, consisting of main and rear, were made of flanged aluminum alloy sheet, with both flap and aileron supports mounted on to the rear spar. The spars were set far enough apart to accommodate the standard aerial armament of the day, the Browning 0.5in machine gun. The barrel of each gun projected through the forward spar. Sufficient space was also provided for one 180 US gallon self-sealing fuel tank, positioned in each inner wing section. The spars were dead straight and were fitted with plate webs and extruded top and bottom booms. Uncomplicated ribs pressed from sheet metal with flanged lightened holes, and extruded span-wise stringers enabled them to carry the large Alclad light-alloy flush-riveted panels. The ailerons were also metal-skinned. Man hours for producing the wing were initially quite high, but as production accelerated, the time fell to two-thirds of that taken to make a Spitfire wing and less than half that for a Hurricane or Typhoon.

26 Squadron was the first RAF unit to receive the Mustang in January 1942 at Weston Zoyland, commencing operations from Gatwick. Mustang Mk I AM148 was one of the first to arrive with the unit before being transferred to 430 Squadron and then a less dangerous role with Rolls-Royce. (Author's Collection)

Undercarriage and systems

Another good feature of the NA-73X was the wide-track undercarriage, which retracted from the outside in like the Hurricane rather than the opposite like the Spitfire and the Bf 109. This immediately gave the advantage of well-spaced wheels, 12ft in the case of the NA-73X, making ground handling easier. The mechanics of the undercarriage were elegantly simple, and, in the retracted position, the wheels were housed in the wing roots, a noticeably forward kink making room for them. Once retracted, the wheels were covered by doors that were hinged from the centerline, and, when extended, were closed again by their own jacks. The tailwheel was equally well-designed, being steerable and linked to the rudder. The unit retracted on pivots and the aperture was neatly closed over by two small doors.

Most US-built aircraft during the 1930s had all-electric systems, but the NA-73X was designed with an all-hydraulic system. An engine-driven pump supplied all sub-systems at various pressures, including the undercarriage, flaps and brakes. However, when armament was introduced to the Mustang Mk I, this was an all-electric system.

Aircraft technical data – Allison-powered Mustangs

Manufacturer: North American Aviation Inc., Inglewood, California, USA

Power	
NA-73X/Mk I/XP-51/P-51 & F-6A	1,150hp Allison V-1710-39 (F3R)
Mk II/P-51A & F-6B	1,120hp Allison V-1710-81 (F20R)
A-26A	1,325hp Allison V-1710-87 (F21R

Dimensions for all Allison variants	
Span	37ft 0.3in (11.29m)
Length	32ft 2.88in (9.83m)
Height	12ft 2in (3.71m)
Wing area	233.19sq. ft. (21.6620m^2)

Weights	
NA-73X	Loaded: 8,633lb (3,924kg)
Mk I/XP-51/P-51/Mk II & F-6A	Empty: 6,300lb (2,863kg) Loaded: 8,600lb (3,909kg)
P-51A & F-6B	Empty: 6,433lb (2,924kg) Loaded: 8,600lb (3,909kg) Max Load: 10,600lb (4,818kg)
A-36A	Empty: 8,370lb (3,804kg) Loaded: 10,700lb (4,863kg)

Performance	
NA-73X	Max speed: 382mph (615km/h) at 13,700ft (4,176m) Range: 750miles (1,200km) Service ceiling: 32,000ft (9,750m)
Mk I/XP-51/P-51A/Mk II & F-6A	Max speed: 390mph (628km/h) at 8,000ft (2,438m) Climb: 8min to 15,000ft (4,572m) Range: 1,050 miles (1,689km) Service ceiling: 32,000ft (9,750m)
A-36A	Max speed: 365mph (587 km/h) Cruise speed: 250mph (402 km/h) Range: 550 miles (885km) (war load) Service ceiling: 25,100ft (7,650m)
P-51A & F-6B	Max speed: 390mph (628km/h) at 12,000ft (1,524m), 360mph (579 km/h) at 15,000ft (4,572m) Climb: 4.4min to 10,000ft (3,048m) Range: 1,050 miles (1,689km) Service ceiling: 31,350ft (9,555m)

Armament	
NA-73X	–
Mk I/XP-51 & Mk II	Four 0.303in. and four 0.5in. Browning machine guns
P-51/Mk IA & F-6A	Four Hispano 20mm guns
A-36A	Six 0.5in. guns, two 500lb (227kg) or on occasion two 1,000lb (454kg) bombs
P-51A & F-6B	Four 0.5in. guns for both plus two 500lbs (227kg) for P-51A

Production					
Model	NAA No.	Contract	Serial	Delivered	Quantity
NA-73X	NA-73		NX19998	Sep 40	1
Mk I	NA-73	A-250	AG345 to AG664	Nov 41 to May 42	320
XP-51-NA	NA-73		41-038 & 41039		2
Mk I	NA-83	A-1493	AL958 to AM257	Apr to Aug 42	200
Mk I	NA-83	A-1493	AP164 to AP263	Jul to Aug 42	100
Mk IA	NA-91	–	FD438 to FD567	Sep 42 to Jan 43	92
P-51-NA	NA-91		41-37320 to 41-37469		148
A-36A-1-NA	NA-97		42-83663 to 42-84162		500
Mk II	NA-99	–	FR890 to FR939	Jun to Jul 43	50
P-51A-1-NA	NA-99		43-6003 to 43-6102		100
P-51A-5-NA	NA-99		43-6103 to 43-6157		55
P-51A-10-NA	NA-99		43-6158 to 43-6312		155

Conversions					
Model	NAA No.	Contract	Serial	Delivered	Amount
F-6A-NA	NA-91	–	–		51
F-6B-NA	NA-99	–	–		35

OPERATIONAL HISTORY

RAF service begins

On January 5, 1942, at Gatwick in West Sussex, 26 Squadron RAF became the first unit to replace its Tomahawks in favour of the Mustang. To cater for the new reconnaissance role, the Mustang was fitted with a port-facing oblique F.24 camera just aft of the cockpit. Many months later, a second, vertically-positioned camera for higher-level survey photography was fitted to many of the Army Co-operation Command's Mustangs. This, combined with the decent firepower of four 0.303 and four 0.5in. machine guns, created a reconnaissance aircraft that could hold its own. Two of the 0.5in. machine guns were mounted below the engine and fired through the propeller, while the remainder were mounted in the wings. The Mustang Mk IA had a much simpler design with four 20mm Hispano Mk II cannons mounted in the wings.

By late February, 26 Squadron had become operational, and, as the amount of airframes arriving in the country quickly increased, other squadrons followed. By May 1942, 2, 4, 16, 255, 239, 241, 268 and 613 (City of Manchester) squadrons had all reequipped with the Mustang. 26 Squadron flew its first operational sortie over France on May 5. The task, which was to set the tone for all of Army Co-operation Command's sorties, was a low-level photo-reconnaissance sortie and was flown by Flying Officer G. N. Dawson in Mustang Mk I AG418 (destined to be lost over Dieppe on August 19,1942). While gaining valuable photography, Dawson headed back low over France crossing the airfield at Berck, where he spotted several vehicles and packing cases. The temptation was too much and Dawson swept back across the airfield, strafing as he went at two hangars in the southeastern corner, before making off at high speed with a large amount of flak and machine-gun rounds in tow. A goods train also received a burst of fire before Dawson made his way back to Gatwick after being in the air for just 1 hour and 40 minutes.

As the capability of the Mustang was quickly realised, these non-aggressive sorties changed into very effective attacks, harassing the enemy in occupied France and into the Low Countries.

Cross-Channel sweeps became a regular event for all of Army Co-operation Command's squadrons, and attacks became more and more daring, so the first operational loss on this type of sortie was not unexpected. While attacking barges near Le Touquet, Mustang Mk I AG415 of 26 Squadron was shot down by ground fire on July 14, 1942, killing 32-year-old Pilot Officer Harold Taylor instantly. It is believed that the fighter flew too low while strafing and struck a barge.

Dieppe and first blood

Throughout early July and into August 1942, many photo-reconnaissance sorties were flown by Army Co-Operation Command in support of the forthcoming Operation *Jubilee*. The brainchild of Lord Louis Mountbatten, the intention of *Jubilee* was to land a large force of Allied troops at Dieppe and hold the port for a short period, to prove it was possible and also to glean any intelligence from the local German forces. Never fully approved by senior military staff, the operation began at 0500hrs on August 19, 1942, with over 6,000 mainly Canadian troops involved. Allied aerial support involved a colossal 70 squadrons of aircraft including virtually all of the operational Mustang units available at the time.

Squadron Leader Charles "Smokey" Stover, the commanding officer of 414 (Sarnia Imperials) Squadron, with his pet dog "Blackie". The photo was taken at Dunsfold in January 1944 during a very intense and successful period of *Rhubarbs* and *Rangers*. (Charles Stover)

The badly-planned invasion was a total disaster and, by 0900hrs, the Allies on the ground were in full retreat. Those in the air fared no better and, by the end of the day, 119 RAF aircraft had failed to return compared to 46 lost by the Luftwaffe. Eleven of these losses were Mustangs, five from 26 Squadron, three from 239, a 400 (City of Toronto) Squadron machine and a pair from 414 (Sarnia Imperials) Squadron. The latter losses included Flight Lieutenant F. E. Clarke RCAF (Royal Canadian Air Force), the wingman of Flying Officer Hollis "Holly" Hills who in AG470 claimed the first enemy kill, a Fw 190, by an RAF Mustang that day. Fred Clarke was attacked by an Fw 190 and ditched in the English Channel from where he was quickly rescued by the Royal Navy. For 26 and 239 squadrons, both based at Gatwick, Operation *Jubilee* was certainly a baptism of fire From the start of the operation, 26 Squadron and 239 Squadron flew 11 and 14 sorties respectively. 26 Squadron operated mainly around the Le Havre, Rouen, Abbeville and the River Somme areas, reporting on troop and enemy transport movements. 239 Squadron also flew low-level tactical reconnaissance of roads from Envernay and Blacy to Le Tréport. Three Mustang pilots survived the day to become POWs. One of them, Pilot Officer A. G. Christiansen RNZAF (Royal New Zealand Air Force) of 26 Squadron, was involved in the mass break out of Stalag Luft III in "The Great Escape" in March 1944. Sadly, he was one of the 50 who were massacred as a result. Hills' success was not the only one on August 19, as a pair of 268 Squadron Mustangs also claimed a Ju 188 destroyed.

RAF Mustangs made history on October 22, 1942 when an unknown unit escorted 22 Wellington bombers on a daylight raid to Germany, thus becoming the first RAF single-seat fighters to fly over the country during World War II. The Wellingtons took part in three separate raids against the Dortmund-Ems canal, the Ruhr, and Essen, all of which were carried out above thick cloud cover. Only 13 of the attacking force actually dropped their bombs but at least one Wellington (possibly influenced by the escorting Mustangs) dropped below the cloud base and machine-gunned a train near Lingen. All of the aircraft returned home safely on this ground-breaking sortie, which proved the usefulness of the Mustang's excellent range and the obvious confidence it gave to the bomber crews it was escorting. By the time the RAF's first order was completed in late 1942, 520 Mustang Mk Is and 92 Mustang Mk IAs had

Flying Officer Hollis "Holly" Hills, an American volunteer flying with 414 RCAF Squadron, was credited with achieving the first Mustang kill over Dieppe on August 19, 1942. Much was made of the fact that Hills was born in Los Angeles, not a million miles from where his aircraft was built. (414 Squadron)

been delivered across the Atlantic (the initial order of 320 was increased by a further 200). Twenty-three squadrons would go on to be equipped with the Mk I, of which six would also operate the Mk IA. As funds began to swell the USAAC kitty again, the need for the dive-bomber variant of the Mustang diminished, with priority changing to a fighter version. The P-51A became the NA-99, with the air brakes removed, and, more significantly, an Allison V-1710-81 with an uprated supercharger and a bigger propeller, improving the aircraft's top speed and giving it marginally higher altitude performance. The uprated engine could propel the Mustang Mk II along at well over 400mph at 10,000ft and the already impressive range was extended to well over 1,200 miles by the new ability to carry drop tanks. The only other significant difference from the earlier marks was the fitting of four 0.5in. guns, but this was to become irrelevant as the development of the Mustang was about to enter a new phase.

E **DIVE-BOMBING IN AN A-36**

Captain Charles E. Dills served in the 522nd FS of the 27th FBG, 12th Air Force in Italy, Corsica and Southern France.

Dills also describes one of the many duties of an A-36 pilot. In dive-bombing

"We were not real close to each other. We stayed a bit open in formation. Each pilot had a duty and could not spend 100 percent of his time looking at the plane whose wing he was flying. When you are that close and look away, you risk an air collision. So we spread out a bit. We flew in groups of four, two two-plane elements. The flight leader did the navigation and spent his time looking forward for various points to keep on course to the target. His wingman was usually on his left and looked ONLY to the right, 100 percent of the time, protecting the flight from attack from the right by enemy aircraft. The element leader flew on the right wing of the flight leader and looked forward and up, again to detect enemy attack from the front and above. He also had to take note of where we were flying in case he had to take over and lead the remaining planes back home. The element leader's wingman looked entirely, 100 percent, of the time to the left, covering the other side of the four-ship formation, giving warning of any imminent attack. The whole formation was a kind of lop-sided V, like four geese! We wanted to avoid any attack because we would have to jettison our bombs. If we did that the enemy would be the winner, even if we were to shoot every one of them down, because they succeeded in protecting our target, and we would have failed in our attack. Dive-bombing was a very focused activity, looking for a specific target. We were usually given an alternate target in case the target was clouded over. If the alternate was also clouded, we could return with the bombs. Of course, if we encountered what the flight leader considered a 'legitimate' target, he would be allowed to dive-bomb it. We did not just jettison the bombs without knowing where they were going. They would be dropped 'safe', meaning they were not supposed to explode if they fell 8,000ft or less. They would still be as dangerous as a 500lb rock!"

A typical dive-bombing attack would take place from around 14,000ft, Dills continues.

"As the group neared the target, the leader waggled his wings. This was the signal to get in trail (single file behind the lead plane). As we got closer to the target, the leader opened his dive breaks and rolled upside down. We flew upside down directly over the target. We then pulled out and went straight down until we had a good sight of the target. I've seen some reports that say we released our bombs at 3,000ft. That's getting a little low. I say we dropped the bombs around 5,000ft or so. As we pulled out, we shut the dive brakes, and it was like getting a kick up the butt. Our speed jumped from 350mph to 450mph, and we got the hell out of there. If there wasn't any flak, we climbed and regrouped for what we were supposed to do next. If there was flak, we just got out of there as fast as we could."

On another operation Dills recounts

"We were attacking some dock, and I had dropped my bombs; I was about to pull out, and there were two bombs flying alongside me! They were no more than 30 or 40ft from me. They must've been dropped by the guy behind me, and I had to fly formation with them until they passed me! They were so close that I could read on the bomb '536 pounds GP!'"

Charles Dills took part in 94 combat missions and flew the A-36 on 39 of them.

Mustang Mk Is of 2 Squadron warm their Allison engines prior to departing on a tactical reconnaissance sortie over Northern France. AG623, the second aircraft along, was lost on May 26, 1943, when it flew into a hill in fog at Kimmeridge in Dorset. (*The Aeroplane*)

'A' for Attack! – The A-36A into combat

It was not until late March 1943 that the A-36A-1-NA began to enter the USAAF, the first recipients being the four squadrons of the 27th Fighter Bomber Group (FBG) under the command of Lieutenant Colonel John Stevenson based at Rasel Ma in French Morocco. Not long after, a second group, the 86th FBG, arrived, which had a full contingent of fully-qualified A-36 pilots on board.

The first operational sorties were flown on June 6, 1943 against the airfields on the islands of Pantelleria and Lampedusa. Following the massed fighter-bomber attack, the islands were captured and became home to the 27th and 86th FBG. The A-36s then supported the Allied landings in Sicily before continuing in the ensuing Italian campaign. Heavy losses were suffered by both groups but the A-36s inflicted equally heavy losses on the enemy, with every conceivable type of target attacked. Troops and vehicles of the Hermann Goering Division were a particular favourite, as were flak batteries and marshaling yards.

A 525th FS, 86th FG A-36A in its natural environment over Mount Vesuvius in early 1944. The aircraft is 42-84081, which was badly damaged in a belly landing at Pomigliano on April 22, 1944. The pilot, Captain Lemeul W. Purdum III, was unhurt. (USAAF)

A US war correspondent reporting on the activities of the A-36 pilots during the campaign wrote the following report:

> The scream of this plane when it dives would shake any man. It makes a Stuka sound like an alley cat. When it levels off at the bottom and lays those bombs right on target, it zooms away as a heavily-gunned fighter, looking for Axis troops to strafe, for enemy planes or tanks or trains to destroy. It's a hot ship ...plenty fast and plenty rugged. No wonder our jubilant pilots nicknamed it "Invader".

The extraordinary accuracy of bombing achieved by the A-36 was demonstrated perfectly on July 31, 1943 when a dozen of the 27th FBG attacked an enemy battery. The battery of four heavy guns was disrupting the advance of US ground forces in Sicily when the group was called in to carry out a strike. A set of accurate coordinates was supplied by the Army, and after being carefully briefed the A-36 pilots took off on the hunt for the enemy positions. On arrival over the position supplied by the Army no guns could be seen, and after the leader circled the position three times, they decided to attack the reference, which was located in an orchard. All 12 A-36s dropped their bombs directly into the orchard and left a little dejected as no sign of the enemy had been seen. However, once the pilots had returned to base they received a congratulatory message from the Army, declaring that all four enemy guns had been silenced.

The A-36 continued to impress. A particular example was on September 10, 1943 when the 27th FBG stopped three German Panzer divisions from getting close to the Salerno beachhead. As a result the 27th FBG earned itself a Distinguished Unit Citation. Another impressive achievement was the sinking of the 50,000-ton *Conti Di Savoia* (Count of Savoy) Italian transport ship at anchor in Baguara Harbour the same month by just two A-36s. The ship, which was a luxurious liner before the war, was later refloated in 1945 but was too far gone to be repaired and was scrapped in 1950.

An A-36A of the 514th FBS, 27th FBG, Twelfth Air Force, mostly likely photographed in Tunisia in 1943. Always officially known as a Mustang, one pilot suggested that the aircraft be named the "Invader" because of the way the type swept from country to country. (USAAF)

A typical rough-and-ready A-36 scene, this time in Sicily in 1943. The aircraft "El Matador" belongs to Flying Officer R. Bryant (left) who is with his crew chief, Sergeant Dan Perry. (USAAF)

It was from the 27th FBG that the first and only Allison-engined Mustang ace came. Lieutenant Michael T. Russo, who was serving with the 16th Bomb Squadron (later 522nd Fighter Bomber Squadron/Fighter Squadron), scored his first aerial victory on September 13, 1943 when his flight was engaged during a dive-bombing attack by a dozen Fw 190s. By December of that year, Russo had become an ace following a successful combat encounter against 16 Bf 109s near Rome, in which he managed to down two of them.

Losses continued to mount, especially as the campaign through Italy began to become more static. German antiaircraft defenses had by now become more organised and these were taking their toll on the two groups' aircraft. By spring 1944, half of the original 150 aircraft that had been assigned to the 27th and 86th FBGs had been lost and their replacements were not forthcoming. Both groups had to reduce their original four squadrons to three, and the A-36s were now being employed on slightly less dangerous tactical fighter work. Strafing and glide-bombing missions were also flown. The latter were far less costly to men and machines than dive-bombing but nowhere near as accurate.

The long endurance time of the A-36 proved its worth during the Salerno landings in September 1943, as the aircraft was able to provide cover over the beachhead up to 30 minutes longer than any other Allied fighter available at the time. A handful of A-36s also served with the 111th TRS in the Mediterranean theater, as well as to replace P-51 losses since there were no replacements for this variant either. In January 1944 the 27th FBG had to revert to the obsolete P-40 as its A-36s were so depleted, having been used to prop up the 86th FBG. It was not until July 1944 that the 86th FBG received the Republic P-47D Thunderbolt, and those A-36s that remained were either scrapped or returned to the US to fly with Mustang training units. The A-36 was a very popular aircraft, as is emphasised by the commander of the Twelfth Air Force, Lieutenant General John K. Cannon, who used one as his personal transport throughout the Mediterranean.

Despite suffering heavy losses (177 were lost in action out of the 500 ordered) the A-36 proved to be a very useful aircraft during the advances from North Africa into Italy. These losses should also be viewed in context of the method of operation the A-36s were flying. As the aircraft were airborne virtually every day, often flying at low level and never far from the sights of enemy guns, these heavy losses seem more understandable.

The type also served with the 311th FBG in India, helping the Allies to push through Burma against the Japanese. Only 40 A-36s were available to the 311th FBG and these were divided into two squadrons, the 528th and 529th FS, while the 530th FS operated the P-51A. Ironically the P-51As had followed the same A-36s assigned to the group straight from the production line. The P-51A was far better suited to the operations to which the 311th FBG was committed, but initially the unit tried to capitalise on having both variants of the Mustang in the field. Both types were used for transport and bomber escort operations, but the deficiencies of the A-36 in one-on-one aerial combat were soon highlighted. On one of the early sorties to provide fighter protection for a formation of C-47s flying from India to China, three A-36s were lost, presumed shot down.

Defining how successful the A-36 was in combat is a little difficult. It was described by some pilots as far too slippery an aircraft to be of any use in the dive-bomber role while others thought the A-36 was highly accurate in the task. A few were lost during training in the early days through structural failure, mainly in the US. Most problems revolved around the dive brakes, which often opened unevenly on the early aircraft, making the A-36 very difficult to control in a dive. Tales of the dive brakes being wired shut are more myth than fact, but it is true that some war-weary machines did have them immobilised as they were not worth fixing.

Postwar statistics compiled by the USAAF on the A-36A revealed that the type flew more 23,000 sorties and, despite being a ground-attack aircraft, claimed 86 enemy aircraft destroyed in air-to-air combat.

A-36A "Bronx Cheer" of the 27th BG gives a nice view of the dive brakes extended and a pair of 500lb bombs in place. Other features of the variant are the early type flame-damping exhausts and early style bomb shackles. (USAAF)

63 mission symbols are displayed on this A-36, which obviously came to grief on its 64th! Even after the belly landing, the dive-bomber's robust undercarriage still functions, but I doubt whether even the resourceful engineers of the USAAF will get this bird flying again. (USAAF)

P-51 in combat

The first operational unit to receive the P-51A was the 311th FBG, closely followed by the 23rd FBG in India. Both of these units were already flying the A-36, so the transition to the latest NAA fighter was uneventful. First operations began on October 16, 1943 but one of the most significant was on November 23 when eight P-51As from Lieutenant General C. C. Chennault's 23rd FG flew escort for a B-25 operation on the Japanese airfield at Shinchiku (now Hsinchu, Taiwan).

Two days later, Mustangs of the 530th FS, 311th FG flew another escort mission in support of a B-25 operation, this time to Mingaladon Airfield, Rangoon. This was the first of three long-range fighter escorts by the newly arrived P-51As and to achieve the extra range a pair of 75 US gallon drop tanks were carried. Round trips were flown from Kurmitola, India, to Rangoon in Burma over 450 miles away; it was these long-range missions that would later become synonymous with the P-51. On this occasion though, the enemy got the better of the US fighters, which were bounced by four Ki-43 Oscars of the highly experienced 64th Sentai, 2nd Chutai based at Mingaladon. A frantic low-level combat ensued at very low altitude, resulting in two Mustangs being shot down.

The next long-range operation was an attempt to escort a formation of Liberators to a target at Insein in Burma. The heavily laden P-51s could not gain much more altitude than the bombers, and as the formation got closer to the target, they were bounced by a gaggle of Ki-43s from the 64th Sentai. One Mustang went down in flames before the pilot had any chance of releasing his drop tanks. In the dogfight that followed, three more P-51s were shot down, including the aircraft of the 311th FG's commanding officer, Colonel Harry Melton. One Ki-43 was shot down and a second had to make a forced landing.

On December 1, 1943, the 311th FBG was ordered to provide the escort for another Liberator operation on Rangoon. Once again, the P-51As struggled for altitude and were outnumbered by the superior Japanese fighters. Another P-51 was shot down, and a second ran out of fuel during the very long flight back via the staging airfield at Cox's Bazaar.

There was no doubt that the P-51A was still far superior to the P-40 and P-38 in one-on-one combat at low and medium altitude, but it was still less maneuverable than the Oscar. Even though the Oscar was under-armed and lacked protective armor, the P-51A always came a poor second during the early aerial battles over Burma. However, the early losses suffered by the 311th FBG were mainly due to lack of experience in comparison to the Japanese. An immediate policy change for the P-51As in engaging the enemy was implemented. All pilots were instructed not to engage in slow-turning combats but to make a high-speed attacking pass instead. The speed gained was to be maintained away from the enemy until a 180° turn could be carried out to reengage. This method of attack was nothing new, having been standard operational procedure for the P-40 pilots and many other Allied fighters for more than two years.

Down and dirty with the 1st Air Command Group (ACG)

Close-support and reconnaissance missions were where the P-51A was at home, and it was with Lieutenant Colonel Philip Cochran's 1st ACG that it excelled. Assigned to provide close support for Major General Orde Wingate's British "Chindits" in Burma, the 1st ACG operated continually from very rough airstrips that had been quickly hacked from the jungle.

A P-51A of the 530th FBS, 311th FBG undergoing minor repairs at Kurmitola, India after combat with Japanese fighters. The P-51s were much valued in China, Burma and India from late 1943, and were used in both air-to-ground and air-to-air roles. (USAAF)

47

Wingate's specialty was his ability to take on the enemy "behind the lines" by using a small, self-sufficient force. This force was reliant on airborne support, as was demonstrated by Wingate's first operations in Burma in 1943, which showed its necessity. The politically well-connected Wingate managed to sweep away all of the red tape and reach Churchill, succeeding in getting a complete air group assigned specifically to support his "Chindits." So the 1st ACG was born to support the troops on the ground, equipped with 13 C-47s, over 200 CG-4A gliders, 12 B-25Hs and at least 100 L-1 and L-5 observation and CASEVAC (casualty evacuation) aircraft. The fighter element, which is where the P-51As came in, would have the multiple role of protecting the transports and bombers while carrying ground-attack missions as well.

An experienced airman who had seen action commanding a P-40 unit in North Africa was chosen to command the unit. Colonel Philip Cochran was just the man to lead the P-51s in action, with Colonel John R. Alison (ex 23rd FG "Flying Tigers") acting as his deputy, although officially they were co-commanders of the 1st ACG. Cochran was quite a character, being the inspiration for the comic-strip character Flip Corkin in "Terry and the Pirates" written by Milton Duff. Both Cochran and Alison brought many highly experienced colleagues with them, including several aces from the Flying Tigers. There was no shortage of talent to fly the fighters over Burma, but there was a distinct lack of P-51s at the time.

Colonel Philip Cochran, the commanding officer of the 1st Air Commando Group, prepares to strap into his P-51A. Cochran was the inspiration for Milton Duff's comic character "Flip Corkin." (USAF)

At this stage of the war, every theater was making justifiable demands for more fighters, but the 1st ACG looked slightly outside the box for its machines, finding several P-51s on training airfields in Florida. The flying over Burma would rarely be at high altitude, making the Allison-powered P-51A the weapon of choice for the ACG. Thirty weary P-51As were requisitioned and sent to India. Their good range, especially with drop tanks from the P-51, made the model ideal to reach the Allied troops, which were far behind enemy lines.

It was February 14, 1944 when Cochran led the 13 P-51As into battle over Burma on the 1st ACG's first mission. The objective was to escort a formation of B-25s on an attack against Japanese facilities at Zaundaing. The ACG fighters joined in the attack by strafing the target, but as they were doing so the Mustangs were bounced by Ki-43s from the 50th Sentai. The veteran Japanese pilots fought very hard, leaving two P-51s shot down and three more damaged. On hearing of the mission, Orde Wingate ordered Cochran to stay on the ground in future, as his loss would be too much to bear.

P-51s and A-36s carried out over 70 sorties against a variety of targets in Burma the same day. Targets included a supply area at Shingban, a military convoy north of Maingkwan, supply dumps and vehicles in the Kamaing area, a bivouac near Mogaung, troops and vehicles between Mogaung and Kamaing, artillery positions at Laawn Ga and a railroad station and warehouses at Lundaung.

The 1st ACG's presence in India raised the morale of the troops on the ground tenfold and Cochran's aggressiveness and ability, as well as his willingness to take risks with his aircraft and pilots in support missions, gained the respect of many serving with the Indian Army. Admiral Lord Louis Mountbatten summed it up by saying, "My boy, you are the only ray of sunshine we have had in this theater this year."

The distinctive five diagonal white stripes of these P-51As give them away as belonging to the 1st ACG. Highly experienced pilots were cherry-picked by Cochran and his deputy Colonel John R. Alison, including several aces from the 23rd FG's "Flying Tigers." (USAAF)

As the ACG gained experience, the tables were slowly turned against the seemingly unbeatable Japanese. Many missions were flown against Japanese airfields that softened up the enemy a fair bit, especially in preparation for the large airdrop and glider Operation *Thursday* on March 5, 1944. This daring operation took place in two large clearings in the jungle, designated "Broadway" and "Chowringee." The first wave saw the 1st ACG's C-47s towing two Waco gliders a way into the two clearings, where the troops on board wasted no time in preparing a pair of landing strips. The following three days saw over 600 C-47 missions, all escorted by P-51s who initially encountered very little opposition thanks to the earlier softening-up operations. A detachment of 1st ACG Mustangs plus several RAF Spitfires made the clearings their home, which were known to have at least three Sentai of

F RAID ON VILLACOUBLAY AIRFIELD, JUNE 29, 1943

By mid-1943, several second-line RAF units had Mustangs on their strength. The AFDU (Advanced Fighting Development Unit) based at Wittering, Northamptonshire had several amongst their diverse range of machines. They also had a huge amount of experience with many of their pilots having seen a great deal of action, a large number in the Battle of Britain. Two characters in particular, Squadron Leader James Archibald Findlay MacLachlan DSO (Distinguished Service Order), DFC (Distinguished Flying Cross) 2 bars, Czech War Cross and Flight Lieutenant Geoffrey Page DFC, had both seen action in the Battle of Britain and the former had served in the defense of Malta. During that conflict, New Zealand-born MacLachlan was struck in the forearm by a cannon shell from a Bf 109 and had to have the arm amputated. This did not stop him from flying as soon as a suitable prosthetic limb was provided, and his exploits flying the Hurricane in the night-intruder role were also well known. Page served with 56 Squadron during the Battle of Britain and was shot down on August 17, 1940, by a Dornier but managed to escape his burning Hurricane. His face and hands were badly burned and Page went on to become one of Sir Archibald McIndoe's famous "guinea pigs" at the Queen Victoria Hospital in East Grinstead.

While evaluating the potential of the Mustang, MacLachlan and Page decided to carry out a more practical exercise on June 29, 1943. Fully fueled and armed, the pair took off from Wittering in Mustang Mk I AM107 and Mustang Mk IA FD442 in broad daylight on a low-level flight to Paris, attacking any target that presented itself. With MacLachlan's false arm firmly clamped to the throttle, the duo approached the enemy training airfield at Villacoublay south of Paris. The weather was overcast over France that day and the Germans were completely caught off guard, with many aircraft practising "circuits and bumps" in the airfield circuit. Within the space of ten minutes, the duo had destroyed six enemy aircraft, four of them Henschel Hs 126s and at least a pair of Junkers Ju 88s on the ground. Page, who claimed two Hs 126s and a Ju 88 shared, described the journey home: "After that, the journey home was uneventful, a kindly rainstorm hid us as we slipped safely over the coast for base and a large tankard of frothing beer!" This really was "boys' own" stuff, but MacLachlan's luck would run out while flying FD442 again on July 18, 1943. It was during a Ranger over France that his Mustang I was hit by ground fire, forcing MacLachlan to make a hasty forced landing. Sadly, he died of his injuries on July 31 and was buried at Pont l'Eveque Communal Cemetery south of Caen.

FD442 was written off that day, but Page's aircraft AM107 went on to enjoy a long and eventful career, being transferred to 285 Squadron based at North Weald in February 1945. A classic example of the longevity of the Allison-Mustang in RAF service, the type still had a part to play even with the war in Europe destined to end a few months later.

Page also went on to a complete and busy career with the RAF, although not before he returned for a further spell of plastic surgery at East Grinstead. He was then posted to 122 Squadron and by January 1944 was commanding 132 Squadron, both units flying the Spitfire. By June, Page was back with 122 Squadron, now its commanding officer, operating from France before being promoted to acting wing commander in charge of 125 Wing. In late September 1944 he was seriously injured following a crash landing, by which time he was credited with shooting down 15 enemy aircraft. After lecturing in the USA in early 1945, Page later joined Vickers-Armstrong at Weybridge as a test pilot, finally settling with that company as a sales executive by the late 1940s.

Japanese fighters based within striking range. Several operations against Japanese airfields were flown from "Broadway" and "Chowringee" over the coming days, including a successful attack on Anisakan Airfield located just off the Mandalay to Lashio road, led by Philippines and Java veteran Lieutenant Colonel Grant Mahoney. This time several Ki-43s were shot down in the air and more than 30 were destroyed on the ground on attacks at Shwebo and Onbauk without loss to the ACG. Further attacks that day saw P-51s return to Shwebo, scoring hits on the runway and dispersal areas, and leaving even more Japanese aircraft out of action. Lieutenant Herbert Krug claimed at least six enemy aircraft destroyed on the ground alone. Krug's luck ran out on March 16, however, when three P-51s were bounced on takeoff by the 50th Sentai. Krug's Mustang was hit and in the ensuing crash landing he was seriously burned, but he survived to be shipped back to the USA.

The attacks throughout March 1944 by the ACG's P-51s were relentless, with communications and transport targets being destroyed by the dozen whilst enemy fighter opposition was being ground down as experienced pilots were running out of luck. However, the whole operation took a knock on March 24, when the B-25H Orde Wingate was flying in ran into bad weather and crashed into the jungle near Bishnupur, Manipur, in northeast India. His replacement, Brigadier Walter Lentaigne, was a completely different soldier and his more cautious approach to tackling the Japanese saw the whole effort lose its momentum.

Regardless, the 1st ACG continued to harry the Japanese forces at every opportunity. One unique method of disrupting communications was employed thanks to Cochran's experiences in Tunisia. The technique was known as cable dragging and was very effective at bringing down telephone wires. The

Mechanics get stuck into a 1st ACG P-51A as part of the aircraft's routine maintenance. As can be seen here, access to the Allison engine was excellent, and complete changes were straightforward compared to many other types. (USAAF)

risky process involved taking off with a long wire rope attached to each wing rack, which trailed far behind the fighter as it climbed into the air. A second wire rope, fitted with small steel weights, was attached to the apex of the loop formed by the first rope. As the rope hung below the Mustang, the steel weights smashed through telephone wires with little difficulty and, on return to the airfield, were released to be used again. Another equally hazardous method of bringing down telephone wires was simply to bank at very low level and use the wing tip to bring the wire down.

It was not until March 25, 1944 that the 1st ACG was officially constituted and activated (on March 29) at Hailakanda, northeast India. This made no difference to the P-51 pilots, who continued their ground campaign the following day, strafing all before them at Anisakan Airfield again. April 4 saw the Japanese begin their ill-fated offensive towards India, which would result in 30,000 enemy dead through disease and starvation alone. More than 120 fighter-bombers of the ACG were in the air on April 4 and the P-51s enjoyed supreme success over the 50th Sentai, which was so badly mauled that it had to be moved to Saigon to reequip.

Additional armament that was often used against the enemy was the standard pair of 500lb bombs, but from February 1944 a pair of 1,000lb bombs was often carried. Three-tube 4.5in M-8 rocket launchers were also carried under each wing, eventually being used by all Mustang units operating in the China-India-Burma theater. One drawback of the rocket launchers was the turbulence they created, which affected the pitot tube pressure. The result could be anything up to a 20mph variation in the indicated air speed, making landing on the small jungle strips even more difficult.

The 1st ACG continued its attacks until May 19, 1944, carrying out its 230th mission that afternoon before being withdrawn for reorganisation. The P-51As of the 1st ACG may have only achieved ten aerial kills, but their skill and getting "down and dirty" saw many more enemy aircraft destroyed on the ground.

Rhubarbs, Rangers and Populars

As the war progressed, the RAF Mustangs were called upon to fly more and more diverse operations including 'Rhubarbs' and 'Rangers'. A Rhubarb, which involved up to four Mustangs, was where a designated target was attacked, generally in France and the Low Countries but, thanks to the aircraft's excellent range, also in Germany. Flown under Fighter Command control, a Rhubarb was never undertaken when the weather was better than 7/10 cloud with a base of 1,500ft, as such a small number of aircraft was always at a disadvantage against enemy fighters. Often described as 'bad-weather' operations, they commenced from October 1942 and continued, when the weather obliged, until the spring of 1944. The targets were wide ranging and included virtually every potential military installation from an airfield to a troop column. The Mustang's field of operations ranged from the Brest Peninsula to the north German coast.

A Ranger, which also comprised a single pair of aircraft, was an extension of a Rhubarb operation and was first introduced in early 1943. These were more free-ranging operations. Thanks to its excellent range, the Mustang was able fully to capitalise on this freedom as it had the ability to operate more than 300 miles from its home airfield. The Hurricane, Spitfire and Typhoon could only manage 210 miles with long-range drop tanks.

A typical Rhubarb or Ranger would be carried out at an average speed of 230mph, increasing to 300mph once over enemy territory. Armed with the element of surprise, losses were comparatively light on these operations, but flying and attacking at low level obviously had its risks. Even when maintaining a high speed, insufficient altitude would be gained to bail out safely if hit, and pilots would often have to ride the crippled machine down to a risky, all too often fatal, crash landing. The target itself could also be dangerous, as is shown by what happened to the popular commanding officer of 4 Squadron, Wing Commander G. E. "Mac" Macdonald on April 28, 1944. Macdonald attacked a munitions barge near Hasselt, which, rather than blowing up immediately, exploded as Macdonald's Mustang passed overhead, killing the pilot and destroying the fighter in an instant. The terrain could also be a problem, as on May 3, 1943 when three out of four 2 Squadron Mustangs were lost. As the quartet returned from a successful strafing attack on rail targets in the Rennes area, the low-flying Mustangs suddenly entered a bank of sea fog. The leader ordered the flight to climb, but by the time they had risen above the fog three of the fighters had crashed into the 150ft high cliffs at St Alban's Head in Dorset.

A 'Popular' was the code name given to low-altitude photographic operations over enemy coastal positions and regions, taking advantage of cloud cover where possible. This was the main type of operations flown by the Army Co-Operation squadrons during the summer and autumn of 1942. Mustangs were also used for shipping reconnaissance work off the Dutch coast in an effort to identify targets for fighter-bombers to attack. How many attacks on enemy shipping actually resulted from this method is not clear. Even Fighter Command occasionally called up the Mustang force, one example being when there was a spate of low-level attacks on south-coast towns by Fw 190s. The long range of the Mustang was also demanded on an increasingly regular basis for both Coastal and Bomber Command escort duties.

All of Army Co-Operation Command's Mustang squadrons took turns flying Rhubarbs, Rangers and Populars. Some were more successful than others, including 268 and 613 squadrons and the two RCAF units, 400 and 414 squadrons. Approximately 30 enemy aircraft were shot down by Allison-engined RAF Mustangs, the majority of them by these four squadrons during their low-level forays across the Continent. The pilots of 400 Squadron alone had also destroyed or seriously damaged over 100 locomotives during their first six months of Rhubarb and Ranger operations. The Canadians also shot down the most enemy fighters, with 12 to their credit. This number increased from June 1943 when the unit began flying night-intruder operations as well.

D-Day, RAF operations

On November 15, 1943, the 2nd Tactical Air Force (TAF) was formed at 'Ramslade', Bracknell, encompassing 2, 83 and 84 groups and 34 Strategic Reconnaissance Wing, all under the control of the Allied Expeditionary Air Force (AEAF). 34 (R) Wing controlled the vast majority of UK-based Mustang Mk I and Mk IAs that were still serving in the low-level reconnaissance role. These aircraft would prove invaluable as the build up to the Allied invasion of Europe gained momentum.

Sortie after sortie was flown from early 1944 onwards, photographing beach obstacles, gradients and coastal features all along the northern French coast. Full use of the oblique camera was made, especially at low level far out

Pilots of 168 Squadron relax between sorties at their temporary home airfield at B8/Sommervieu, just behind the Normandy beachhead, two miles northeast of Bayeux. Operating from northern France meant that the long-range Mustangs could penetrate even deeper into enemy territory. (Author's Collection)

to sea and looking towards the coast. Photography was taken at approximately 3½ miles out to sea at very low level, giving prospective captains and coxswains of assault craft a good idea of what they would be heading towards. Further obliques were taken at about 1,500 yards from the coast to help platoon commanders and shots were taken at 2,000ft from a similar position to give a view of the assault area's hinterland. Various areas and objects further inland, including bridges, riverbanks and various defensive positions were also carefully photographed.

Alongside photo-reconnaissance de Havilland DH-98 Mosquitoes and Spitfires, the RAF's Mustangs left no stone unturned. Even the Allied invasion force itself was continually photographed to make sure its own protective camouflage was working. During the fortnight leading up to June 6, 1944, one RAF mobile photographic lab printed nearly 120,000 photographs. From April 1 to June 5, 1944, all AEAF tactical fighter-reconnaissance aircraft flew 3,215 photographic sorties. There would be no excuse for not having up-to-date intelligence of the landing areas.

The first task allotted to the RAF Mustangs on D-Day itself was spotting for naval gunners, a task that would continue until midday. Mustang Mk IA FD546 and FD562 of 268 Squadron from Gatwick and Mustangs Mk IA AG529, AM104, AG548, and AP213 of 414 Squadron, Odiham were the first airborne from 0455hrs. Of the 81 'spotting' sorties flown by the three squadrons (including 2 Sqn with Mustang Mk IIs) taking part that morning, only one 2 Squadron machine, FR924, was damaged by enemy antiaircraft fire, and still returned home safely.

The first tactical-reconnaissance sorties of the day also started before the sun was up. At 0500hrs, two Mustangs of 168 Squadron, flown by Flying Officer J. A. Lowndes in AM102 and Flying Officer E. Winiars in AM197, were airborne first from Odiham, heading south at low level towards the Normandy beaches. 430 (City of Sudbury) Squadron, also based at Odiham, was the second Mustang unit to join the fray. A pair of aircraft left for France at 0505hrs. Both of these squadrons continued to dispatch Mustangs

The commanding officer of a Mustang squadron oversees the fitting of a fully-loaded F.24 oblique camera for a sortie over Normandy. The camera was accessed from the starboard side of the rear cockpit and the lens pointed to the port. (Author's Collection)

throughout the day, and from 0825hrs they were joined by aircraft from 268 Squadron as well. It is possible that the 268 Squadron machines operated from Lee-on-Solent in Hampshire throughout June 6, which would be logical as it would give the aircraft even more time to operate over the beachhead. Light antiaircraft fire was the main threat, but the first Mustang victim of the day fell to the guns of the Allies. Mustang Mk I AM225 of 168 Squadron, which had set out for the Ouistreham area, was hit by gunfire from an Allied warship and blew up off Lion-sur-Mer. The pilot was 22-year-old Flying Officer Stanley Harry Barnard who hailed from Recife, Pernambuco in Brazil. He was killed instantly. Mustang Mk I FD495 of 268 Squadron, with Flight Lieutenant E. D. Woodward at the controls, also fell victim to colossal Allied naval bombardment.

By mid-afternoon, enemy air activity was on the increase and 430 Squadron probably encountered more than any other Mustang unit that day. Flying Officer Gordon in AG664 and Flying Officer Lambros in AM253 came across six Junkers Ju 88s, but the combat that took place, if any, is inconclusive. Later in the day, the officer commanding 430 Squadron, Wing Commander Godfrey in Mustang Mk I AM103 and Flying Officer J. S. Cox in AG465 were providing cover for Squadron Leader Chester in AP186 while he undertook a tactical reconnaissance sortie. While approaching the Evreux area, the three aircraft were bounced by four Fw 190s, one of which shot Cox down almost immediately. Two other Fw 190s joined the fray, and both Godfrey and Chester wisely decided to head for the clouds and set course for Le Havre, hotly pursued by at least one Fw 190, which managed to score a few hits on Chester's aircraft. Cox became the third and final Mustang pilot to be killed that day, which, although tragic, was a very low casualty rate considering the nature of their work. Eighty-eight tactical reconnaissance sorties were flown by 2, 168, 268 and 430 Squadron on June 6, providing the Allied commanders with a continuous stream of photographic images that would continue as the invasion progressed. 430 Squadron would average 400 sorties a month post D-Day.

A host of units

By the time the last batch of Mustang Mk IIs was delivered in July 1943, the RAF had 27 operational squadrons flying one of the Allison-powered breed. Forty-two second-line units can be credited with flying the three marks, some more prolific than others, including 41 OTU (Operational Training Unit) based at Old Sarum, Wiltshire. Formed in September 1941, the OTU was already responsible for training pilots in the art of low-level tactical reconnaissance, initially on the Westland Lysander and the Tomahawk. The first Mustangs arrived in April 1942 and by July an establishment of 43 aircraft had been created. After moving to Hawarden in north Wales in November 1942, the Mustang remained the dominant type until the Hurricane took over from mid-1944. By the end of 1944, use of the Mustang had petered out at 41 out, but it continued to serve with several front-line squadrons until August 1945, with 268 Squadron at Hustedt in Germany being the last.

Pilots of 2 Squadron share a joke over a letter in one of the lighter moments of life on an operational squadron. As with all units, there were hours of inactivity mixed with adrenaline-inducing, low-level, high-speed flying over enemy territory. (Author's Collection)

One of the last aircraft in USAF service still to be powered by Allison engines was the F-82E (P-82E) Twin Mustang. The aircraft entered service in 1948 and had the unique capability of being able to fly from London to Moscow with drop tanks, loiter over the target for 30 minutes, and then fly home. (USAAF)

Several Mustangs remained with second-line units well into 1947; the very last was Mustang Mk I AG357. This long-serving machine was one of the first to be trialed by the A&AEE at Boscombe Down before being moved to the RAE at Farnborough. After a brief spell with 595 Squadron, AG357 returned to the RAE and was SOC until July 31, 1947 after providing nearly six years of uninterrupted service.

The Allison's second wind – the Lightweight and Twins

XP-51J

The Allison engine made a surprise comeback in early 1945 during the testing and development of the lightweight series of Mustangs. The result of this testing led to the USAAF ordering the P-51H (NA-126) in April 1944, but further testing was still ordered on an Allison-powered lightweight, designated the XP-51J.

The XP-51J was destined to be the last of the lightweights. Two aircraft were procured under the original NA-105 designation, which also called for the XP-51F and XP-51G. It may seem surprising that the Allison engine was chosen, but by this stage of its development it was a completely different unit compared to the 1940 version. The latest Allison was the V-1710-119, a highly-developed version of the original engine with a two-stage supercharger like a Merlin and water injection to increase boost. The engine was rated at 1,720hp with war emergency power at 20,000ft, but the Allison never achieved these figures and was restricted to 1,500hp during flight testing. Installation was very neat with no chin intake being present, making for a very smooth profile, and an Aeroproducts four-blade propeller was also fitted.

Just two XP-51Js were built, 44-76027 and 44-76028, the former being flown the first time by test pilot George Welch on April 23, 1945. The latter first took to the air in the hands of George Krebs on January 29, 1946, by which time there was no demand for such an aircraft. The full potential of the XP-51J was never realised because of the restriction in horsepower, although in theory the aircraft should have reached, if not breached, 500mph at 20,000ft. Allegedly both aircraft were turned over to the USAAF in February 1946, but this may have been shortlived as they were later passed on to Allison at Indianapolis for engine-development work. It was this development work that led to another Allison powering a rather different version of the Mustang family.

P-82E/F-82E Twin Mustang

Born from a requirement of the USAAF for a very long-range escort fighter, the P-82 Twin Mustang had been on Edgar Schmued's design board since 1940. The concept was a lot more than two Mustang fuselages bolted to a long wing, as the aircraft was virtually a new concept from the ground up. The fuselages were based on a pair of P-51H lightweights, but even these were extended by 57in. from behind the cockpit.

Four prototypes, two XP-82s powered by Packard Merlin V-1650s and two XP-82As powered by the XP-51J's Allison V-1710-199, were ordered in early 1944. Only one of the Allison machines, 43-83888, was built, first flying on August 30, 1945. This was fortuitous for the P-82 program as a whole because, with the end of World War II, the end of licensed manufacture of the Rolls-Royce Merlin engine brought supply into doubt. The end of the war also brought about extensive cutbacks, and an initial order for 500 V-1650-powered P-82Bs was dropped to just 20 aircraft.

Two night-fighter versions, the P-82C and P-82D, were converted from the original batch, but a big order was back on the table for an escort-fighter version, designated the P-82E (NA-144). An order for 500 aircraft was placed, all of them to be powered by the Allison V-1710-143/145, which may have been for a combination of two reasons. Firstly, as mentioned earlier, Rolls-Royce had by now revoked its license and Packard would have to pay a $6,000 royalty per unit built. Secondly, many American manufacturers were suffering because of the massive military cutbacks that occurred during the postwar period, and the USAAF order attempted to keep both Allison and NAA in business.

The 1,600hp V-1710-143/145s were not the most reliable of engines, often being described as the "Allison time bomb" because of regular failures. The trouble and modification work they caused made the $6,000 demanded by Rolls-Royce for the Merlin more than worth it. When the engines were running properly, the F-82E (it changed from P for Pursuit to F for Fighter from mid-1948) was a very pleasant aircraft to fly and the performance was excellent, even on one engine. Only 100 F-82Es were built and the first entered service with the 27th FW (Fighter Wing) at Kearney AFB (Air Force Base), Nebraska in March 1948.

The final member of the Allison-powered family was one of the unmistakable night-fighter versions of the Twin Mustang family, the F-82G. The appearance of this version was dominated by a large SCR-720C radar pod that was fitted to the bottom of the mid-wing. Power was again provided by a pair of V-1710-143/145s, which provided 1,600hp each on takeoff, although the power could be raised to 1,930hp at sea level when a water/alcohol mix was injected for short bursts. The F-82G could reach just under 460mph at 21,000ft and had a colossal range of over 2,200 miles. Only 50 F-82Gs were built, although it proved to be a very useful aircraft with many of them acting as an interim replacement for the P-61 Black Widow before the arrival of jet night-fighters. The F-82G served with distinction in Korea, and on June 27, 1950, three of them claimed a Lavochkin La-7 and La-11 and a Yakovlev Yak-9, the first air-to-air kills made by a Twin Mustang. By 1952, the short service career of the Twin Mustangs had come to an abrupt end and the Allison's second wind was over.

CONCLUSION

Even in its original form, despite the limitations of the Allison engine, the Mustang's performance was very good. It was popular with all who flew it and no less popular with those who kept it flying. The aircraft was originally ordered as an air superiority fighter for the RAF's Fighter Command, but it was clear that the aircraft's strength was "down on the deck," and it was here that the type excelled. Many Air Co-Operation pilots had been flying the P-40 Tomahawk or even the Lysander before the arrival of the Mustang. The increased range was a godsend and the increased speed a bonus, and in addition the ability to fight back when necessary was something to which the RAF pilots were not accustomed.

A real treat for aviation enthusiasts in Britain was the arrival of the Chino-based A-36 42-83731/N251A at Duxford's Flying Legends in 2002. (Author's Collection)

ALLISON-POWERED SURVIVORS

Across the globe 165 P-51s survive in airworthy condition, a further 58 are on display, 45 are under restoration, 23 are in storage and seven are unaccounted for. Of these, just nine are Allison-powered variants and only four of those are airworthy (although a fifth is in the pipeline), making these very rare warbirds indeed.

41-038/N51NA – The original XP-51 is on display at the EAA Aviation Foundation, Oshkosh, Winnebago, Wisconsin. After being saved from the scrap man in 1949, the fighter was restored to flight in 1976, only to be retired again in 1982.

42-83665/N39502 – The A-36 "Margie H" was built in October 1942. The fighter was on the civilian register by 1946 and was entered into the Kendall Trophy Race the following year, finishing in second place. In 1972 the owner, Charles Doyle, traded the aircraft to the USAF Museum, Dayton, Ohio, where it remains to this day. The code 'N39502' has since been allocated to a Bell UH-1B.

42-83731/N251A – This A-36 was restored to flying condition by Thomas Camp in 1975 and was one of the stars of Flying Legends at Duxford in 2002. This event marked the first time an A-36 had been seen in Britain since the end World War II. Rebuilt at Chino in 2003, the fighter was back in the air by 2010. It is based at Chino, California.

42-83738/N4607V – As of 2012, the aircraft is approaching the final assembly stages of a restoration project by the Collings Foundation at New Smyrna Beach, Florida.

43-6006/N51Z – The P-51A-10NA "Polar Bear" was delivered to Mines Field on April 3, 1942, followed by allocation to Ladd Field, Fairbanks, Alaska, for service with the USAAC. Unfortunately, the fighter crashed near Summit Alaska on February 16, 1944, killing the pilot, Lt Edward W. Getter. In 1977 Waldon "Moon" Spillers recovered the wreckage, and an eight-year restoration followed, resulting in the fighter flying again on July 3, 1985. Since 2005 this P-51A has been one of the stars of the Reno Air Races and still puts in good performances considering it is entered as a "stock" machine.

43-6178/N51KW – This P-51A-10NA has been changing hands since 1950 until finally settling with Kermit Weeks in 1981. Registered as N51KW in 1984, the fighter is currently in storage at the Weeks Air Museum, Polk City, Florida, where it is awaiting restoration.

43-6251/N4235Y – The P-51A-10NA "Mrs Virginia" has been with the Planes of Fame Air Museum since 1981, having previously been owned by Cal Aero Tech and Ed Maloney, who spent many years restoring the fighter. It got back into the air on August 19, 1981, and is today one of the many warbird performers on the US air show circuit.

43-6274/N90358 – This P-51A-10NA has been owned by Charles Nichols at the Yanks Air Museum since 1978 and, after a lengthy restoration, was finally completed in 1993. The fighter is on display, in pristine condition, at the Yanks Air Museum, Chino, California.

N8082U – The P-51A "Precious Metal II" is a new airframe that was constructed in 2001 and registered to Gerald S. Beck of Wahpeton, North Dakota, as N8082U on March 31, 2006. The aircraft was completed by May and named "Precious Metal II". On July 27, 2007, at the EAA Airventure, Oshkosh, after carrying out a mock air race with several other warbirds, Gerry's aircraft touched down behind a P-51D, struck its tail and turned over on its back. Sadly, Gerry was killed but on January 12, 2010, the registration of "Precious Metal II" was transferred to his wife, Cynthia, and work began on restoring the P-51 to fly again in his memory.

Although entering service almost a year after the RAF, it was the A-36 that began to arrive in numbers with the USAAF in North Africa first. A truly underrated aircraft, it performed well in a role it was never intended for and continued to do so until the aircraft or spares ran out. In the Far East, the P-51A was always at a disadvantage against the superior Japanese aircraft, but tactics and sheer blood and guts would eventually prevail.

Not enough credit is given to Allison-engined variants of one of the world's most famous fighters. There is no doubt that the Merlin elevated the Mustang's performance from being "very good" to "exceptional," and this, in many people's eyes, peaked with the P-51B and P-51C, not the more familiar and most produced version, the P-51D, that we see more often today. In total, 1,723 Allison-powered Mustangs were built, but only a handful survives today compared to the Merlin-powered machines. One of the survivors is the original XP-51 41-038, which was rescued from the scrap man by the Smithsonian National Air & Space Museum in 1949. Restored to flight and registered as N51EA, the XP-51 returned to the skies in 1976, only to be sadly retired again in 1982. This rare machine is now on static display with the Experimental Aircraft Association at Oshkosh, Wisconsin.

A-36 42-83731/N251A at rest at Duxford. This was the first time an A-36 had been seen in Britain since the end of World War II. (Author's Collection)

FURTHER READING

Bowyer, J. F., *Aircraft For The Many*, PSL (1995)

Cull, B., and Symons, R., *One-Armed Mac*, Grub Street (2003)

Franks, L. R., *RAF Fighter Command Losses of the Second World War 1942-1943*, Midland Publishing Ltd (1998)

Freeman, Roger A., *Mustang in Combat*, Ian Allan Ltd (1974)

Gruenhagen, R. W., *The Story of the P-51 Fighter*, Arco (1976)

Gunston, B., and Dorr, R. F., *North American P-51 Mustang*, Aerospace Publishing Ltd (1995)

Halley, J. J., *RAF Aircraft AA100 to AZ999*, Air Britain (2000)

Halley, J. J., *RAF Aircraft FA100 to FZ999*, Air Britain (1989)

Hamlin, J. F., *Support and Strike!*, MGS (1991)

Johnson, B., & Heffernan, T., *A Most Secret Place*, Jane's (1982)

Jefford, C. G, *RAF Squadrons*, Airlife (1993)

Lowe, M. V., *North American P-51 Mustang*, Crowood (2009)

Pearcy, A., *Lend-Lease Aircraft in World War II*, Airlife (1996)

Shores, C. F., *2nd Tactical Air Force*, Osprey (1970)

P-51A-10NA "Polar Bear"
at the 2005 Reno Air Races.
(Author's Collection)

INDEX

Page numbers in **bold** show illustrations.